: @ 1 – for

° upon 1st – cannot

disparaging → discouraging

° Plimpton's awareness

~~its~~ the

In a way... ~~its~~ we

Praise for

The Man in the Flying Lawn Chair

"In true Plimptonian fashion, it's a cocktail party of a book, 18 pieces jostling against each other in a crowded smoky space. . . . Even on assignment, Plimpton seems to have had more fun than writers are normally allowed to have. And yet he must have worked very hard at writing, because prose so elegant and offhand and constructed with such seeming effortlessness could have only arisen out of hard labor."

—*The New York Times Book Review*

"The subjects of the pieces are themselves fascinating. . . . For a writer who so often places himself in the middle of his work, the strongest pieces here are those where Plimpton is least intrusive."

—*Booklist*

"*The Man in the Flying Lawn Chair* . . . is not unlike its late author: erudite in manner, endearing in tone, an elegant anomaly in a world so often characterized by its lack of grace and charm. . . . Every part [is] perfectly balanced and . . . full of endless charm."

—*BookPage*

"Plimpton's infectious, offbeat eye and breezy prose are inimitable. . . . This book provides a fitting farewell to the man known as the Paper Lion—who didn't merely live it up, but wrote it down with grace, wit and feeling."

—*New York Post*

Also by GEORGE PLIMPTON

The Rabbit's Umbrella (juvenile)
Out of My League
Writers at Work: The Paris Review *Interviews*, Volumes I–IX (ed.)
Paper Lion
The Bogey Man
American Literary Anthologies, Volumes I–III (ed.)
American Journey: The Times of Robert F. Kennedy (with Jean Stein)
Pierre's Book (ed.)
Mad Ducks and Bears
One for the Record
One More July
Shadow Box
Sports (with Neil Leifer)
A Sports Bestiary (with Arnold Roth)
Edie: An American Biography (with Jean Stein)
D.V. (with Christopher Hemphill)
Fireworks: A History and Celebration
Open Net
The Curious Case of Sidd Finch
Poets at Work : The Paris Review *Interviews* (ed.)
Women Writers at Work : The Paris Review *Interviews* (ed.)
The Best of Plimpton
Chronicles of Courage (with Jean Kennedy Smith)
The Writer's Chapbook
The Paris Review *Anthology* (ed.)
The Norton Book of Sports (ed.)
The X Factor
Truman Capote
Playwrights at Work : The Paris Review *Interviews* (ed.)
Pet Peeves, or, Whatever Happened to Doctor Rawff?
Home Run (ed.)
Latin American Writers at Work: The Paris Review *Interviews* (ed.)
As Told at the Explorers Club: More Than Fifty Gripping Tales of Adventure (ed.)
Ernest Shackleton

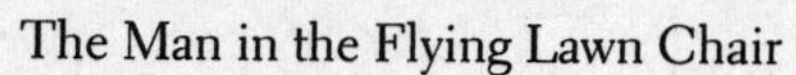

The Man in the Flying Lawn Chair

Random House Trade Paperbacks

New York

GEORGE PLIMPTON

The Man in the Flying Lawn Chair

and Other Excursions and Observations

EDITED BY

Sarah Dudley Plimpton

2005 Random House Trade Paperback Edition

Published in the United States by
Random House Trade Paperbacks,
an imprint of The Random House Publishing Group,
a division of Random House, Inc., New York.

RANDOM HOUSE TRADE PAPERBACKS and
colophon are trademarks of Random House, Inc.

Originally published in hardcover in the
United States by Random House,
an imprint of The Random House Publishing Group,
a division of Random House, Inc., in 2004.

LIBRARY OF CONGRESS
CATALOGING-IN-PUBLICATION DATA

Plimpton, George.
The man in the flying lawn chair :
and other excursions and observations /
George Plimpton.
p. cm.
ISBN 0-8129-7372-0
I. Title.
PS3566.L5M36 2004
814'.54—dc22 2004048117

Printed in the United States of America

www.atrandom.com

2 4 6 8 9 7 5 3 1

Book design by Barbara M. Bachman

Contents

Introduction

—

George Plimpton left us all rather suddenly last September, on the eve of the fiftieth-anniversary celebration of his beloved *Paris Review.* With his passing, a light went out and the world became just a little bit duller. Who would entertain us with feats of derring-do, fireworks, musings, and revelry? Who would tell those wonderful, absurd stories that could entertain us for hours? Who would make us laugh at ourselves?

Last summer George and his assistant, Tom Moffett, began compiling some of his recent writing into a collection. The job has since passed to me, and I hope readers will find in this eclectic mix something of his sensibility. While I was searching for material, I came across a computer file dated the morning he passed away. I quickly pulled it up, desperate to find out what had been on his mind. His entry could well serve as an epigraph for this volume.

Perhaps he even meant it as such. It was a quote paraphrasing André Gide:

> The trouble with a life too well planned
> is that it leaves little room for adventure.

That was George. He saw life as a colorful series of capers, and kept a running list of new escapades long after most men his age would have been content to sit back and reflect. The more absurd the adventure, the better. Why else would he search out the man who launched himself into the stratosphere above Los Angeles International Airport supported only by a dime-store lawn chair and weather balloons? Or submit himself to the athletic rigors of the Olympic-training facility in search of a sport ideally suited to his storklike physique? Or plan a children's treasure hunt replete with pirates pulling ashore in a longboat, a wooden chest filled with jewels and treasure, and a plank-walking thrown in for good measure?

Thank heaven for the crackpots, screwballs, pursuers of dreams—George loved them all.

Sarah Dudley Plimpton
July 8, 2004

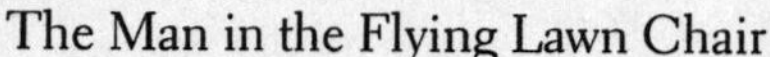

The Man in the Flying Lawn Chair

The Man in the Flying Lawn Chair

—

The backyard was much smaller than I remembered—barely ten yards by thirty. The birdbath, stark white on its pedestal, was still there, under a pine tree, just as it had been during my last visit, more than ten years before. Beyond the roofs of the neighboring houses I could see the distant gaunt cranes of the Long Beach naval facility, now idle.

"Mrs. Van Deusen, wasn't there a strawberry patch over here?" I called out.

I winced. Margaret Van Deusen has been blind since last August—first in one eye, then in the other. Her daughter, Carol, was leading her down the steps of the back porch, guiding her step by step. Mrs. Van Deusen was worried about her cat, Precious, who had fled into the innards of a stand-up organ upon my arrival: "Where's Precious? She didn't get out, did she?"

Carol calmed her fears, and my question about the strawberry patch hung in the air. Both women wore T-shirts with cat motifs on the front; Mrs. Van Deusen's had a cat head on hers, with ruby eyes and a leather tongue.

We had lunch in a fast food restaurant in San Pedro, a couple of miles down the hill. Mrs. Van Deusen ordered a grilled cheese sandwich and french fries. "I can't believe Larry's flight happened out of such a small space," I said.

Mrs. Van Deusen stirred. "Two weeks before, Larry came to me and said he was going to take off from my backyard. I said no way. Illegal. I didn't want to be stuck with a big fine. So the idea was he was going to take off from the desert. He couldn't get all his equipment out there, so he pulls a sneaker on me. He turns up at the house and says, 'Tomorrow I'm going to take off from your backyard.' "

"I was terrified, but I wanted to be with him," said Carol, who was Larry's girlfriend at the time.

"And sit on his lap?" I asked incredulously.

Two chairs, side by side," Carol said. "But it meant more equipment than we had. I know one thing—that if I'd gone up with him we would have come down sooner."

"What happened to the chair?" I asked.

Carol talked in a rush of words. "He gave it away to some kid on the street where he landed, about ten miles from here. That chair should be in the Smithsonian. Larry always felt just terrible about that."

"And the balloons?"

"You remember, Mom? The firemen tied some of the balloons

to the end of their truck, and they went off with these things waving in the air as if they were coming from a birthday party."

"Where are my fries?"

"They're in front of you, Mom," Carol said. She guided her mother's hand to the sticks of french fries in a cardboard container.

Mrs. Van Deusen said, "Larry knocked some prominent person off the front page of the *L.A. Times*, didn't he, Carol? Who was the prominent person he knocked off?"

Carol shook her head. "I don't know. But that *Times* cartoonist Paul Conrad did one of Ronald Reagan in a lawn chair, with some sort of caption like 'Another nut from California.' Larry's mother was upset by this and wrote a letter to the *Times*. You know how mothers are."

I asked Mrs. Van Deusen, "What do you remember best about the flight?"

She paused, and then said she remembered hearing afterward about her five-year-old granddaughter, Julie Pine, standing in her front yard in Long Beach and waving gaily as Larry took off. "Yes. She kept waving until Larry and his chair were barely a dot in the sky."

It was in all the papers at the time—how on Friday, July 2, 1982, a young man named Larry Walters, who had served as an Army cook in Vietnam, had settled himself into a Sears, Roebuck lawn chair to which were attached four clusters of helium-filled weather balloons, forty-two of them in all. His intent was to drift northeast in the prevailing winds over the San Gabriel Mountains to the Mojave Desert. With him he carried an air pistol, with which to pop the balloons and thus regulate his altitude. It was an ingenious solution, but in a gust of wind, three miles up, the chair tipped, horrifyingly, and the gun fell out of his lap to the ground, far below. Larry, in his chair, coasted to a height of sixteen thousand five hundred feet. He was spotted by Delta and TWA pilots taking off from Los Angeles Airport. One of them was reported to have radioed to the traffic controllers, "This is TWA 231, level at sixteen thousand feet. We have a man in a chair attached to balloons in our ten o'clock position, range five miles." Subsequently, I read that Walters had been fined fifteen hundred dollars by the Federal Aviation Administration for flying an "un-airworthy airworthy machine."

Some time later, my curiosity got the better of me, and I arranged to meet Larry Walters, in the hope of writing a story about him. "I was always fascinated by balloons," Larry began. "When I was about eight or nine, I was taken to Disneyland. The first thing when we walked in, there was a lady holding what seemed like a zillion Mickey Mouse balloons, and I went, 'Wow!' I know that's when the idea developed. I mean, you get enough of those and they're going to lift you up! Then, when I was about thirteen, I saw a weather balloon in an Army-Navy surplus store, and I realized that was the way to go—that I had to get some of those big suckers. All this time, I was experimenting with hydrogen gas, making my own hydrogen generators and inflating little balloons."

"What did you do with the balloons?" I asked.

"I sent them up with notes I'd written attached. None of them ever came back. At Hollywood High School, I did a science project on 'Hydrogen and Balloons.' I got a D on it."

"How did your family react to all this?"

"My mother worried a lot. Especially when I was making rocket fuel, and it was always blowing up on me or catching fire. It's a good thing I never really got into rocketry, or I'd have probably shot myself off somewhere."

"Did you ever think of just going up in a small airplane—a glider, maybe—or doing a parachute jump to—"

"Abolutely not. I mean no, no, no. It had to be something I put together myself. I thought about it all through Vietnam."

"What about the chair?"

"It was an ordinary lawn chair—waffle-iron webbing in the seat, tubular aluminum armrests. Darn sturdy little chair! Cost me a hundred and nine dollars. In fact, afterward my mother went out and bought two of them. They were on sale."

I asked what Carol had thought of his flight plans.

"I was honest with her. When I met her, in 1972, I told her, 'Carol, I have this dream about flight,' and this and that, and she said, 'No, no, no, you don't need to do that.' So I put it on the back burner. Then, ten years later, I got a revelation: 'It's now or never, got to do it.' It was at the Holiday Inn in Victorville, which is on the way from San Bernardino to Las Vegas. We were having Cokes and hamburgers. I'm a McDonald's man: hamburgers, french fries, and Coca-Cola, for breakfast, lunch, and dinner—that's it! Anyway, I pulled out a quarter and began to draw the balloons on the place mats."

"What about Carol?"

"She knew then that I was committed. She said, 'Well, it's best you do it and get it out of your system.' "

A few months before the flight, Larry drove up to the Elsinore Flight School, in Perris, California. He had agreed, at Carol's insistence, to wear a parachute, and after a single jump he bought one for nine hundred dollars.

"Didn't that parachute jump satisfy your urge to fly on your own?" I asked.

"Oh, no, no, no, no, no!" he said.

Other essentials were purchased: a two-way radio; an altimeter; a hand compass; a flashlight; extra batteries; a medical kit; a pocketknife; eight plastic bottles of water to be placed on the sides of the chair, for ballast; a package of beef jerky; a road map of California; a camera; two liters of Coca-Cola; and a BB gun, for popping the balloons.

"The air pistol was an inspired idea," I said. "Did you ever think that if you popped one, the balloon next to it would pop, too?"

"We did all these tests. I wasn't even sure a BB shot would work, because the weather balloon's rubber is fairly thick. But you can pop it with a pin."

"Did your mother intervene at all?"

"My mother thought maybe I was possessed by the Devil, or perhaps post-Vietnam stress syndrome. She wanted me to see a psychiatrist. We started inflating the day before, at sundown—one balloon at a time, from fifty-five helium cylinders. Each balloon, inflated to about seven feet in diameter, gets a lift of about twelve pounds—the balloons would have lifted about a quarter of a ton. Around midnight, a couple of sheriff's deputies put their heads over the back wall and yelled, 'What's going on here?' I told them we were getting ready for a commercial in the morning. When the sun came up the next morning, a lot of police cars slowed down. No wonder. The thing was a hundred and fifty feet high—a heck of an advertising promotion! But they didn't bother us."

The flight was delayed for forty-five minutes while one of Larry's friends ran down to the local marine-supply store and bought a life jacket in case there was a wind shift and he was taken out to sea. At ten-thirty, Larry got into his lawn chair.

I asked whether he had worn a safety belt—a silly question, I thought.

But, to my surprise, Larry said he hadn't bothered. "The chair was tilted back about ten degrees," he said, illustrating with his hands.

The original idea was that Larry would rise to approximately a hundred feet above the Van Deusen house and hold there, tethered by a length of rope wrapped around a friend's car—a 1962 Chevrolet Bonneville, down on the lawn—to get his bearings and to check everything out before moving on. But, rising at about eight hundred feet per minute, *Inspiration*—as Larry called his flying machine—reached the end of the tethering rope and snapped it; the chair pitched forward so violently that Larry's glasses flew off, along with some of the equipment hanging from the chair.

That was quite enough for Carol. Larry had a tape of the conversation between the two of them on the two-way radio. He put it on a tape deck and we sat and listened.

Her voice rises in anguish: "Larry, come down. You've got to come down if you can't see. Come down!"

Larry reports that he has a backup pair of glasses. His voice is calm, reassuring: "I'm A-OK. I'm going through a dense fog layer."

Predictably, this news dismays Carol: "Oh, God! Keep talking, Larry. We've got airplanes. They can't see you. You're heading for the ocean. You're going to have to come down!"

When Larry reaches twenty-five hundred feet, she continues to cry into the radio set, "Larry, everybody down here says to cut 'em and get down now. Cut your balloons and come down now. Come down, please!"

The tape deck clicked off.

I asked Larry how he had reacted to this desperate plea.

"I wasn't going to hassle with her," Larry said, "because no way in heck, you know, after all this—my life, the money we'd sunk into this thing—and just come down. No way in heck. I was just going to have—have a good time up there."

"What was it like?"

"The higher I went, the more I could see, and it was awesome. Sitting in this little chair, and, you know, Look! Wow! Man! Unreal! I could see the orange funnels of the *Queen Mary*. I could see that big seaplane of Howard Hughes's, the *Spruce Goose*, with two commercial tugs alongside. Then, higher up, the oil tanks of the naval station, like little dots. Catalina Island in the distance. The sea was blue and opaque. I could look up the coast, like, forever. At one point, I caught sight of a little private plane below me. I could hear the 'bzzz' of its propeller—the only sound. I had this camera, but I didn't take any pictures. This was something personal. I wanted only the memory of it—that was vivid enough.

"When I got to fifteen thousand feet, the air was getting thin. Enough of the ride, I thought. I'd better go into a descent and level off. My cruising altitude was supposed to be eight or nine thousand feet, to take me over the Angeles National Forest, past Mount Wilson, and out toward Mojave. I figured I needed to pop seven of the balloons. So I took out the air pistol, pointed up, and I went, 'pow, pow, pow, pow, pow, pow,' and the balloons made these lovely little bangs, like a muffled 'pop,' and they fell down and dangled below my chair. I put the gun in my lap to check the altimeter. Then this gust of wind came up and blew me sideways. The chair tilted forward, and the gun fell out of my lap! To this day, I can see it falling—getting smaller and smaller, down toward the houses, three miles down—and I thought, I hope there's no one standing down there.

"It was a terrifying sight. I thought, Oh-oh, you've done it now. Why didn't you tie it on? I had backups for most everything. I even had backup BBs in case I ran out, backup CO_2 cylinders for the gun. It never dawned on me that I'd actually lose the gun itself."

I asked if the gun had ever been found.

Larry shook his head. "At least, no one got hit."

"Imagine that," I said. "To be hit in the head with a BB gun dropped from three miles up."

"That's what the F.A.A. talked about," Larry said. "They told me I could have killed someone."

"Well, what happened after you dropped the gun?"

"I went up to about sixteen thousand five hundred feet. The air was very thin. I was breathing very deeply for air. I was about fifteen seconds away from hauling myself out of the chair and dropping down and hoping I could use the parachute properly."

I asked how high he would have gone if he hadn't popped the seven balloons before he dropped the gun.

Larry grimaced, and said, "At the F.A.A. hearings, it was estimated that I would have been carried up to fifty thousand feet and been a Popsicle."

"Was that the word they used?"

"No. Mine. But it was cold up where I was. The temperature at two miles up is about five to ten degrees. My toes got numb. But then, the helium slowly leaking, I gradually began to descend. I knew I was going to have to land, since I didn't have the pistol to regulate my altitude."

At thirteen thousand feet, Larry got into a conversation on his radio set with an operator from an emergency rescue unit.

He put on the tape deck again. The operator is insistent: "What airport did you take off from?" He asks it again and again.

Larry finally gives Carol's mother's street address: "My point of departure was 1633 West Seventh Street, San Pedro."

"Say again the name of the airport. Could you please repeat?"

Eventually, Larry says, "The difficulty is, this is an unauthorized balloon launch. I know I am interfering with general airspace. I'm sure my ground crew has alerted the proper authorities, but could you just call them and tell them I'm OK?"

A ground-control official breaks in on another frequency. He wants to know the color of the balloons.

The balloons are beige in color. I'm in bright blue sky. They should be highly visible."

The official wants to know not only the color of the balloons but their size.

"Size? Approximately seven feet in diameter each. And I probably have thirty-five left. Over."

The official is astonished: "Did you say you have a cluster of thirty-five balloons?" His voice squeaks over the static.

Just before his landing, Larry says into the radio set, "Just tell Carol that I love her, and I'm doing fine. Please do. Over."

Larry clicked off the tape machine.

"It was close to noon. I'd been up—oh, about an hour and a half. As I got nearer the ground, I could hear dogs barking, automobiles, horns—even voices, you know, in calm, casual conversation."

At about two thousand feet, *Inspiration* suddenly began to descend quite quickly. Larry took his penknife and slashed the water-filled plastic bottles alongside his chair. About thirty-five gallons started cascading down.

"You released everything?"

"Everything. I looked down at the ground getting closer and closer, about three hundred feet, and, Lord, you know, the water's all gone, right? And I could see the rooftops coming up, and then these power lines. The chair went over this guy's house, and I nestled into these power lines, hanging about eight feet under the bottom strand! If I'd come in a little higher, the chair would have hit the wires, and I could have been electrocuted. I could have been dead, and Lord knows what!"

"Wow!"

Larry laughed. "It's ironic, because the guy that owned the house, he was out reading his morning paper on a chaise longue next to his swimming pool, and, you know, just the look on this guy's face—like he hears the noise as I scraped across his roof, and he looks up and he sees this pair of boots and the chair floating right over him, under the power lines, right? He sat there mesmerized, just looking at me. After about fifteen seconds, he got out of his chair. He said, 'Hey, do you need any help?' And guess what. It turns out he was a pilot. An airline pilot on his day off."

"Wow!" I said again.

"There was a big commotion on the street, getting me down with a stepladder and everything, and they had to turn off the power for that neighborhood. I sat in a police car, and this guy keeps looking at me, and he finally says, 'Can I see your driving license?' I gave it to him, and he punches in the information in his computer. When they get back to him, he says, 'There's nothing. You haven't done anything.' He said I'd be hearing from the F.A.A., and I was free to go. I autographed some pieces of the balloons for people who came up. Later, I got a big hug and a kiss from Carol, and everything. All the way home, she kept criticizing me for giving away the chair, which I did, to a kid on the street, without really thinking what I was doing."

"So what was your feeling after it was all over?"

Larry looked down at his hands. After a pause he said, "Life seems a little empty, because I always had this thing to look forward to—to strive for and dream about, you know. It got me through the Army and Vietnam—just dreaming about it, you know, 'One of these days. . .' "

Not long after our meeting, Larry telephoned and asked me not to write about his flight. He explained that the story was his, after all, and that my publishing it would lessen his chances of lecturing at what he called "aviation clubs." I felt I had no choice but to comply.

I asked him what he was up to. He said that his passion was hiking in the San Gabriel Mountains. "Some people take drugs to get high. I literally get high when I'm in the mountains. I feel alive. I've got my whole world right there—the food, my sleeping bag, my tent, everything."

—

Larry's mother, Hazel Dunham, lives in a residential community in Mission Viejo, California, forty miles southeast of San Pedro. The day before seeing the Van Deusens, I dropped in on her and Larry's younger sister, Kathy. We sat around a table. A photograph album was brought out and leafed through. There were pictures of Larry's father when he was a bomber pilot flying Liberators in the Pacific. He had spent five years in a hospital, slowly dying of emphysema. Larry was close to him, and twice the Red Cross had brought Larry back from Vietnam to see him. After his father's death—Larry was twenty-four at the time—his mother had remarried.

"Do you know Larry's favorite film—*Somewhere in Time*?" Kathy asked.

I shook my head.

"Well, one entire wall of his little apartment in North Hollywood was covered with stills from that picture."

"An entire wall?"

Both of them nodded.

"It's a romantic film starring Christopher Reeve and Jane Seymour," Kathy said. "It's about time travel."

She went on to describe it—how Christopher Reeve falls in love with a picture of a young actress he sees in the Hall of History at the Grand Hotel on Mackinac Island. From a college professor, he learns how to go back in time to 1912 to meet her, which he does, and they fall in love. But then he's returned to the present. He decides he can't live without her and at the end they're together in heaven.

Kathy turned back to the photograph album. "Look, this is a picture of Larry's favorite camping spot, up in Eaton Canyon. A tree crosses the stream. I'll bet Larry put his Cokes there. He'd have a backpack weighing sixty pounds to carry up into the canyon, and I'll bet half of that was Coca-Cola six-packs."

"I bought cases of it when he took the train down here to visit," his mother said.

"Here's a picture of Larry in his forest-ranger uniform," Kathy said. "He was always a volunteer, because you have to have a college degree to be a regular ranger. He loved nature."

"And Carol?"

"They sort of drifted apart. They were always in touch, though." She turned to another page of the album. "Here's the campsite again. See this big locker here, by the side of the trail? It was always locked. But this time it wasn't. They found his Bible in there."

"He fell in love with God," his mother said. "He was always reading the Bible. When he was here last, he smiled, and said I should read the Bible more. He marked passages. He marked this one in red ink in a little Bible I found by his bed: 'And ye now therefore have sorrow: but I will see you again, and your heart shall rejoice, and your joy no man taketh from you.' "

She looked at her daughter. Her voice changed, quite anguished, but low, as if she didn't want me to overhear. "Drug smugglers were in the area, Kathy. Larry was left-handed, and they found the gun in his right hand."

"Are you sure, Mom?"

"That's what I think, Kathy. And so does Carol."

"There were powder burns on his hand, Mom."

"I guess so," Mrs. Dunham said softly.

Kathy looked at me. "It's OK for Mom to believe someone else did it. I think Larry never wanted to give anyone pain. He left these hints. He stopped making appointments in his calendar."

Her mother stared down at the photo album. "Why didn't I pick up on things when he came down here to visit me? I just never did."

Not long ago, I spoke over the telephone to Joyce Rios, who had been a volunteer forest ranger with Larry. "I turned sixty last year," she told me. "I started hiking with Larry into the San Gabriel Mountains about eight years ago. He was always talking about Carol when I first met him. 'My girlfriend and I did this' and 'My girlfriend and I did that.' But after a while that died down. Still, he was obsessed with her. He felt he was responsible for their drifting apart. He felt terribly guilty about it."

Joyce went on. "We had long talks about religion, two- or three-hour sessions, in the campsites, talking about the Bible. I am a Jehovah's Witness, and we accept the Bible as the Word of God—that we sleep in death until God has planned for the Resurrection. I think he was planning what he did for a long time. He left hints. He often talked about this campsite above Idler, in a canyon below Mount Wilson, and how he would die there. He spent hours reading Jack Finney's *Time and Again.* Do you know the book? It's about a man who is transported back into the winter of 1882. They tell him, 'Sleep. And when you wake up everything you know of the twentieth century will be gone.' Larry read this book over and over again. In the copy I have he had marked a sentence, from a suicide note that was partly burnt. Here it is: 'The Fault and the Guilt [are] mine, and can never be denied or escaped. . . . I now end the life which should have ended then.' "

After a silence, she said in a quiet voice, "Larry never called the dispatcher that day. We knew something was wrong. I hiked up to the campsite with a friend. The search-and-rescue people had already found him. I never went across the stream to look. I couldn't bear to. I was told he was inside the tent in his sleeping bag. Everything was very neat. His shoes were neatly placed outside. The camp trash was hanging in a tree, so the bears and the raccoons couldn't get to it. He had shot himself in the heart with a pistol. His nose had dripped some blood on the ground. His head was turned, very composed, and his eyes were closed, and if it hadn't been for the blood he could have been sleeping."

Back in New York, I rented a video of *Somewhere in Time.* It was a tearjerker, but what I will remember from it is Christopher

Reeve's suicide. He wants to join Jane Seymour in heaven. Sitting in a chair in his room in the Grand Hotel on Mackinac, where in 1912 his love affair with Jane Seymour was consummated, he stares fixedly out the window for a week. Finally, the hotel people unlock the door. Too late. Dying of a broken heart or starvation (or possibly both), Reeve gets his wish. Heaven turns out to be the surface of a lake that stretches to the horizon. In the distance, Seymour stands smiling as Reeve walks slowly toward her; he doffs his hat and their hands touch as the music swells. No one else seems to be around—just the two of them standing alone in the vastness.

The New Yorker,
JUNE 1, 1998

Exeter Remembered

—

I think I should start off by saying that I didn't do very well at Exeter. In fact, I was a complete failure. I was asked to leave three months shy of graduation because of a multitude of sins, both academic and secular. My teachers couldn't take it anymore and I was sent away, down to my grandparents in Ormond Beach, Florida. I spent those three months at the Daytona Beach High School, so I could get a diploma and move on to Harvard, where I had already been accepted.

The principal there was interesting. He could throw a baseball equally hard off either wing, truly ambidextrous, which was to be admired since I doubt your [Exeter] principal, Mr. Tingley, can do such a thing, even on a good day. The principal taught me Greek for three months and I sashayed into the Great Hall of the Lampoon Building at Harvard, where I should have been all along.

A few years ago, I was looking at television and suddenly discovered the national cheerleading competition was going on. There were pyramids of girls in pert skirts and in the finals, what's more, the Daytona Beach cheerleading team! I sat there mesmerized, calling out "Hey! Hey!" from time to time, and doggoned if they didn't win. I was thinking of sending them a telegram, but I'd been there for such a short time, and so long ago, almost sixty years, that it probably wouldn't have meant anything to them.

In any case, I bring you greetings from the Daytona Beach High School!

Thus I come to you as sort of an outsider, as if you were being addressed by Satan, once an archangel, but then tossed out of Heaven.

What went wrong with me at Exeter? It may have been because I was too young. I was ten when I arrived that fall. Well, that's not quite true. I was about right—fourteen years old, but as innocent as if I were ten. I knew nothing about anything.

In the old days, prior to the big Andover game, the student bodies from both schools used to line up on either side of Front Street and raise three cheers for the opposing school's principal. Andover's fellow was a man named Fuess, and we would draw out the *s*, snakelike, to suggest what we thought of him: *"Fuessssss! Fuessssss! Fuessssss!"* They would then come back with three cheers for Lewis Perry, our guy, whose name they were coached to say, quite sharply and distinctly, *"Fairy! Fairy! Fairy!"*

I didn't know it was a derogatory remark. I thought it was rather sweet—the thought of Lewis Perry, a rather robust gent, being referred to as something quite sylvan and rather romantic, like a character in *A Midsummer Night's Dream.* It wasn't until I got to Cambridge University that I realized the Andover people, far more sophisticated than I was, were referring to something quite different.

Detention, Probation, Study Hall

My marks were terrible. I had the strange idea that in class, even if I were daydreaming of something else, my brain was still absorbing all the material like a kind of specialized sponge, and the next day at the exam I could scratch around in the appropriate corner, in the detritus, and there would be the appropriate answers. Of course it didn't work that way, and my marks, the Cs, the Ds, the occasional E—the latter always in math—showed it.

These elicited letters from my father—the only letters I ever got, with his familiar, dreaded handwriting—and they were stiff with reprimand. He was Exeter, his brother was Exeter, his father was Exeter: George Arthur Plimpton, class of 1873, gave the playing fields, raised funds for Phillips Church. Though my father never actually said as much, I was truly letting down the side. Genetically speaking, I was supposed to soar through Exeter. Wasn't the family tree full of outrageous successes? There were generals, senators, tycoons, empire builders, college presidents, lawyers, poets—including the *first* American poet, Edward Taylor (unreadable, I might add). And now, at the end of the line, like a caboose with two wheels missing, dragging along the ground, shooting up sparks and igniting forest fires, *this.* My father wrote a weekly letter in which the operative word was "apply," as in "you really must apply yourself." All of this must have also worried my mother—even though she knew perfectly well that there hadn't been an indiscretion that would have resulted in this infant manqué. At the end of vacation, I would assure her and Father: "I will apply myself." Then I would march north immediately into detention, probation, study hall, where you went if your marks were too low.

I was confined a lot, like a caged mink. As I sat there in study hall, I would think up titles to the books I would write: *The Blue Locomotive. The Riders of the Purple Hills. The Dead Man of Deadman's Gulch.* I had been hooked on Zane Grey ever since reading *Riders of the Purple Sage.* From the public library on Front Street, as I recall, I took out dozens of such volumes, when I should have been reading the books I'd been assigned for class. Why wasn't there an exam on *Riders of the Purple Sage*? Instead it was Tacitus, the Roman historian. What were his views on Vespasian? "Get out your pencils, please. Potter, pass out the blue books." Sometimes I thought I was in the wrong classroom.

I used to sit in study hall and curse my brain. I used to imagine taking it out of the top of my head and beating it sharply with a pencil. Why had it let me down? True, I hadn't studied, but why hadn't my brain compensated properly out of thin air? Somewhere in Melville's *Moby Dick* is the line "my whole beaten brain seems as beheaded." Which is apt, thinking back on it, because my head, when I was at Exeter, was ever off somewhere else, funning it up with the heads of the few others who were having difficulty. We beheaded few, we band of brothers.

At nightfall, I went down to the Plimpton Playing Fields and drop-kicked field goals with Buzz Merritt, just the two of us in the gloaming, often with a thin moon shining above the pines, above the river. No one drop-kicks footballs now, or did then either. Why did I do this when I should have been studying Tacitus for the exam I knew was coming up the next day? Buzz got away with it somehow, but I didn't. Sometimes, to escape the exams, I went to the infirmary. There was a secret way, which I've now forgotten, to drive up the temperature on a thermometer. If you were careless, you could drive it up to 110 degrees. I always thought Dr. Fox somehow knew, perhaps by the panicky face he was looking at, what the true trouble was, and he would put you in the infirmary for the day.

When I wasn't on detention, or probation, or sitting in study hall, I spent, at least in my final years, a great deal of time in an institution one can hardly believe existed—the butt rooms, where one learned to smoke. There was more smoke in one of those rooms than there is in the funnel of an old-fashioned locomotive. We sat in there and we were suave. I'm surprised we didn't wear green eyeshades and hats. At night I would lie in bed and, in the moonlight streaming through the window, practice blowing smoke rings. As they oozed thickly up toward the ceiling, I'd say to myself, Wow! If only Susie Mills—the girl who had a driver's license and drove her father's Plymouth with the top down—could see me now!

But what really got me into trouble were the little things I thought were funny—like sneaking in at night and turning all the benches around in the Assembly Hall because I thought it would be funny to have my classmates sitting backwards when they came in for assembly.

In Phillips Hall, there was a large room with a collection of stuffed animal heads hanging on the wall. The Zoo, it was called then, although the animal heads are no longer there, I've been told, because of political correctness problems. For reasons that seem unfathomable to me now, I thought it would be amusing to remove the rhino head and put it somewhere else—say, the stage of the Assembly Hall, where it would look out on the student body gathered for assembly.

I was, of course, caught with the rhino head. *Mortification.* What do you say if you're caught with such a thing? Afterward, but too late, the thought occurred to me that I should have said, "I'm bringing it back."

I had a friend when I was at Cambridge University who stole a tiny Modigliani statue from the Tate Gallery, because, as he said, he liked it a lot and wanted to spend some time with it. After a while, he went to London and returned it. Modigliani wasn't very well known at the time, so there wasn't much of a fuss. He told me about this my second year there, and I said, "Well, that's all very well, but I took a rhino head off the wall and tried to put it in the Assembly Hall." I'm not sure he believed me, and I'm not sure I believed him, but he became a great newspaper editor afterward and very distinguished.

When I was at Exeter, a friend of mine at Groton turned all the pipes around in the organ loft as a prank, so that when the organist sat down to play a good, fervid, high-Episcopal hymn such as "Nearer My God to Thee" or "Onward, Christian Soldiers," out came a bar or two of Schoenberg. If I had heard of this at the time, I would have hastened off to Phillips Church, wrench in hand, and tried to do the same.

I would have been caught. I was caught all the time. It was as if I were attached to an invisible leash at the other end of which was an authority of some kind. I'd be called in to see Dean Kerr in his offices. Shuffling in and asked to explain myself, I would open my mouth—and nothing would emerge. Sometimes in answer to a probing question of his ("Why did you think to move that stuffed rhino head?"), I would murmur, head down, "Yessir." I never looked at Dean Kerr. I didn't dare. Out of sight, out of mind. I didn't know what he looked like. "Oh, look," someone would say, "there's Dean Kerr." "Who?" I would reply. "Where?"

Try, Try Again

I wanted so much to succeed, to make a noise. I wrote for the *Exonian*, but if you were on probation you couldn't use your real name. My pen name was "Vague," thought by many to be my state of mind most of the time. I wrote a column and got into trouble because I made up items about famous Exeter graduates ("Who *was* that woman seen with Robert Benchley at the Stork Club?"). What on earth prompted me to write such a thing? Dean Kerr called me in. He knew I wrote under the name "Vague"; he knew everything. "Yessir," I said, looking at my feet.

I tried out for varsity sports. Bill Clark, the baseball coach, never took the care to find out that he had a youth, "a barefoot boy with cheek," who could throw a lazy, roundhouse curveball. I was cut. Football, the same. Hockey, the same. Tennis, the same. Tall as a reed, fragile as a stick, I ended up in the band playing the bass drum. What a little group we had back there! Ted Lamont carried the drum, as I recall, on his back like a mammoth papoose, while I went along behind him, whacking it with a big felt-covered hammer. Buzz Merritt played the cymbals; Jake Underhill, the snare drum. Jake was telling me the other day that the younger kid who played the snare alongside him has just retired from his position as chief judge of the Massachusetts Supreme Court.

I tried other things. I took piano lessons from Mr. Landers. He assigned me a Debussy piece called "Bells," as I recall. I went down to the practice rooms, which were located under Phillips Church and which had just enough room in each for a stand-up piano and a seat. The walls were paper thin, so you could hear five other pianos going at the same time. The next week I appeared at Mr. Landers' quarters and sat down to play. Mr. Landers said, "Well, that's very fine, but that's not Debussy's 'Bells.' "

I tried drama. I tried out for a play called *Seven Keys to Baldpate*. They found a minor role for me, that of a young widow. My part was, to put it mildly, small—one line or so and then I was required to let out an unearthly scream, perhaps at the sight of a corpse, I've forgotten what. I did so—unleashed a high-pitched vocal effort that blasted the drama coach, John Mayher, back in his chair. My scream carried far out over the quadrangle, down the hill past Langdell and into the Jeremiah Smith Building, past the mailroom with its letter boxes—where in those days I received only my father's letter, once a week, with its admonitions—and up the stairs to Dean Kerr's office, where he sat comfortably smoking his pipe, when suddenly this high-pitched shriek wandered in, and his blood curdled and he said aloud, "*My God, what's Plimpton done now?*"

So I was in a play. I wore a dress. It wasn't bad. Someone took a picture and I sent it to my father to show him that I was applying myself. I've always had the suspicion that he took it to my mother and said, "Look what you've done."

Girls

There were no girls in Exeter at the time. The nearest girls were in Montpelier, Vermont. So the big thing was the spring dance. Susie Mills came up by train. She carried a little suitcase. She was put up someplace. She came out and we walked around. It was like being with Dean Kerr. I didn't know what to say to her. We wandered about like figures in a Fellini film. I was in and out of my *Riders of the Purple Sage* mode, and I walked slightly bowlegged. I said I was going to be a cowhand for the summer. "Is that so," she said after a while. She was so pretty I didn't dare look at her for fear my heart would jump out of my body. "Would you like to hear me play Debussy's 'Bells'?" I asked. She said she didn't see why not.

I led her down into the cellar of Phillips Church where the music rooms were. My heart was in my throat. "In here," I said huskily. I closed the door, soundproofed so that it closed with a slight *whoosh.* "Would you like a Camel?" I said. "I smoke Camels these days, though this summer I intend to roll my own."

"Is that so." She took one.

"You inhale," I said, surprised. She let out a thin stream of smoke that went by my ears, and then coughed. We played with smoke the way children play with toys.

I oozed a smoke ring out over her head, reached past her shoulder and switched off the light. Instant, stygian blackness except for the two fireflies of our cigarette ends.

Just then, in the practice room next door, there was a crash of piano keys, as if someone had sat abruptly on the keyboard. Spennie Welch was in there, I knew, because he had told me as much, that he was going to be in there with his date, a girl who was rumored to have been accepted by Vassar. Tall, red-haired girl. Wore a red-dyed mink boa to match. In there I heard what sounded like a slap, followed by a shout, dim, through the wall: "What do you think you're doing!"

In my own compartment, suddenly and thunderously, not more than an inch from my ear in the pitch darkness, Susie Mills called out, "Turn on the light!" Fumbling desperately against the wall, my hand sweeping it with great arcs, I found the light switch, and the little room blazed with light. And we stared shocked at each other.

I asked Spennie Welch about it a couple of evenings later . . . in the butt room. He had his feet up on the table, leaning back, a Camel cigarette in his mouth. The place was full of smoke. Spennie hadn't learned to inhale. Many of us hadn't. We puffed the stuff out, Bill Clinton–style. So I asked him, "Well, how'd it go, pard?"

"How did what go?"

"The Vassar woman?"

He puffed and coughed. "A walk in the park," he said. He was very blasé, and talked like that.

"And you?" he asked.

"We had a right good time," I lied. I thought of her getting on the train with her little suitcase, never looking back.

I have always thought, in fact, that one learns as much from one's peers at school as one does from the teachers. I recall writing a story which received a C−. It was a story based on a curious ritual that used to be one of the features of Sports Day at St. Bernard's School in New York City—an occasion held out in the country somewhere. One of the last races of the afternoon was the chauffeur's race—these being the long-gone days when a large number of boys (present company excluded) were delivered to the school by large black Packards and picked up by same. Many of the chauffeurs, an astonishing number, almost as many as raced in the fathers' race, competed on Sports Day, lining up their black shoes at the starting line and racing in their black stockings.

My story was about a young girl from the Chapin School who adored the family chauffeur—a portly gent, Perkins in name, as I recall—in the way young girls fall in love with large dogs. She had pleaded with him to run in the chauffeurs' race, which, against his better judgment, he had done. Halfway through, he keeled over and that was it. The poignant conclusion of my story found the Chapin girl leaning over him and saying something like, "Oh, Perkins, how could I have done this to you?"And this came back with a C− and such comments as "Unconvincing. Improbable. Watch overuse of exclamation points."

Toby Wherry, of pleasant memory, happened to read my story. Quite angrily, ripping the paper with his eraser, he tried to rub out the C− and replace it—not with an A, but an A−, because perhaps he wasn't sure of it himself.

Gore Vidal was a class ahead of me. He was so persuaded of his own abilities way back then that he sent in his own pieces to the school's literary magazine, the *Review*, signing them with a fictitious name, perhaps that of a first year boy who lived in Dunbar, and then sat at the editorial meeting glorying in the praise heaped by other editors on what was actually his own work ("Who *is* this kid?").Vidal later read a long, epic free-verse saga of mine about being lost in the Exeter woods one night, far beyond the river. Although the other editors dismissed it out of hand, he wrote me a note or spoke to me about it—a faint note of praise, but it was like a thunderclap from above.

There is always an epiphany when you think about wanting to write, and that (and Toby Wherry's A−) was surely one of them.

And I Owe It All to Exeter

My main nemesis was Bill Clark, who taught math (E-) and was the football and baseball coach. He was the master of Soule Hall where I lived that senior year. One night I was chasing Spennie Welch down the curved stairs with a flintlock musket my grandfather had given me—a relic of the Revolutionary War. As I was going down, suddenly, around the curve of the wall, on his way up to see what all the commotion was, came Bill Clark, also referred to as "Bull." He gave this little scream. I don't really blame him. The barrel end of the musket looked like the mouth of a tunnel. A fair-sized rocket could have emerged from it. I knew I was doomed, as Holden Caulfield would say. If he had toughened it out and said, "What are you doing with that flintlock musket when you should be in your room applying yourself?," it would have been all right. But he had given this little scream, and he knew that I knew, and I knew that he knew that I knew. And that was it.

Could it have been that, having failed in all departments at Exeter, I was driven in later life to compensate, to try once again to succeed where I hadn't? I've wondered, on occasion, whether these exercises in participatory journalism for which I am known were as much to show my mentors at Exeter that I had somehow managed to intrude onto the highest plateaus of their various disciplines.

In the 1970s, I played for the Baltimore Colts against my old team, the Detroit Lions, in an exhibition game in Ann Arbor in front of 103,000 people, the largest crowd ever to see a professional game up until that time. I was sent in for four plays as their quarterback and while I was in there we made eighteen yards, fifteen of them on a roughing-the-passer penalty. Old Bill Clark, I bet he'd never run onto the football field in front of 103,000 people. No, sirree. I daydreamed at the time that in his pep talk before the Andover game, that year, he said, "We've got a great tradition here. Got a guy playing in pro ball. So go out there and make him proud."

Nor do I think that Bill Clark ever stood on the pitcher's mound in Yankee Stadium in a postseason All Star game and looked down on the likes of Willie Mays. I threw my big, sweet roundhouse curveball and Mays popped the ball up—out by the monuments in deep center field—but the ball was caught and he was out. True, later on, Frank Thomas of the Chicago White Sox hit the longest home run seen in the stadium all that summer, up in the triple tier—so far, in fact, that I felt that I'd been a partner in quite an engineering feat. Look what he and I had done together! I wonder if Bill Clark wouldn't have traded for that. He was also the hockey coach. We had tryouts on the frozen Exeter River—a race, and I came in last. What could he have thought when he learned that I played goal for the Boston Bruins?

Mr. Rogers was the tennis coach. I played tennis against Bobby Riggs. True, Bobby was playing while wearing Wellington boots and had a dachshund on a leash as a weird kind of handicap, but I could pride myself in that Mr. Rogers, the tennis coach, had never played Bobby Riggs.

I wonder if John "Call me John" Mayher ever knew, having relegated me to the role of a young widow, that I have been in three Oscar-winning films—*Lawrence of Arabia,* in which I played a Bedouin; Warren Beatty's *Reds,* in which I tried unsuccessfully to seduce Diane Keaton, probably because of my unfortunate experience with Susie Mills in the bowels of Phillips Church; and *Good*

Will Hunting, in which I played a psychiatrist accused of being gay. I'm not trying to suggest that these films wouldn't have received Oscar nominations if I had not been involved, but I see no harm in suggesting that is indeed so.

I like to think that John Mayher did know of these minor triumphs, at least the early ones, and that just before the curtain went up at Exeter he called his cast together around him: "Boys," he says, "give it your all. We have a reputation to live up to. An Exeter boy made it to Tinseltown. You can do as well. Break a leg!"

And music. I wish Mr. Landers could have known I played the piano at the Apollo Theater in Harlem—on amateur night, which is held every Wednesday, a great tradition which has produced the likes of Nina Simone and Dinah Washington. I was allowed to compete so that I could write about the Apollo and its history firsthand. The audience is the judge.The place is packed, and if they don't like what's going on, they stomp their feet and hoot, and out comes the hook in the form of a personage called the Great Adam, firing a pistol and dressed, at least in my day, in a union suit. He removes the contestant to the wings, while the audience hollers and carries on.

My debut at the Apollo was a rock-and-roll night. The guy who preceded me played some rock and roll on an old-fashioned teakettle, blowing across the spout and banging the teakettle lid on the top, a one-man-band sort of thing, and it wasn't more than half a minute before the Great Adam came out, firing his pistol, and the teakettle man was escorted off. So I went out, touching the trunk of a tree just offstage for good luck. The emcee was Honi Coles, the great tap dancer. I was dressed in a business suit. "Well, what are you going to do?" Honi Coles asked. "I am going to play the piano," I said. "And what is the name of the composition you will be playing?" I thought of saying Debussy's "Bells," but then I thought there might be somebody in the audience who would recognize that it wasn't Debussy's "Bells" and might make mention of the fact, prompting the pistol-firing entrance of the Great Adam. So I said, "It's called Opus No. 1." "Opus No. 1," Honi Coles announced, and I sat down at the grand piano (whose keys had been touched by the fingers of Duke Ellington and Fats Waller and such), and I played Opus No. 1.

And guess what. Despite some rumblings of discontent at music which sounded less like Debussy's "Bells" than the background music to *The Edge of Night*, I managed to survive the entrance of the Great Adam, and indeed won second prize, losing out to a young girl who tap-danced to the tune of "Dancing Shoes."

They call the Apollo "the stepping-stone to the stars," and I like to think of Mr. Landers at a lesson, leaning back and saying, "Young man, I had a student once, liked to play Debussy cadenzas. Made it to the Apollo Theater. Practice, young man, practice!"

I wonder if Mr. Bennett—who taught English and may or may not have been the one who gave me a C− for the story about the chauffeurs' race—ever knew that I ran a literary magazine and occasionally wrote books and magazine pieces, mostly about mavericks and people who remind me slightly of myself.

As for all my Cs, Ds, and Es, I'm not sure this is a vindication, but eventually I ended up at Cambridge University, Kings College. At Cambridge, there are no exams until your final year, and then there are two weeks of exams, held in June but referred to (typically English) as "the Mays"—three hours in the morning, three hours in the afternoon. There is one exam you can't study for: the essay. You are asked to write for three hours on whatever question is proffered.

The question was: Write (in so many words) on Charles James Fox. I didn't know who Charles James Fox was. If I'd applied myself at Exeter, if my head hadn't been off with its pals, funning it up, I would have known. But I didn't. We all should know, actually. Fox was a member of Pitt's cabinet, a strong supporter of the American position at the time of the Revolutionary War, an eccentric, a compulsive gambler, and so on. But I didn't know this. So after half an hour or so, I picked up my pencil and wrote as follows: "Charles James Fox was a mediocre second baseman for the Cincinnati Reds," and went on about this completely imaginary figure for the rest of the exam. And guess what. I eventually got an honors degree—a low one, I must admit, but still.

Now at Exeter, Mr. Bennett would have slapped an E on there, and "watch the overuse of commas and exclamation points," and that would have been that.

I have come to the conclusion that my life, whatever there is of it that might be termed successful, was indeed very much due to Exeter's credit . . . that I had somehow to vindicate myself. And I am grateful for Exeter, terribly grateful, and I wish my grandfather had never given me that flintlock musket.

"Thy sons to the jubilee throng." It's a call that suffices here at this annual gathering, whichever institution came up with that line, Harvard actually. And so it is good to come back. I am very glad to have thronged to this jubilee.

The Exeter Bulletin,
SPRING 2002

My Life with *Playboy*

—

Hugh Hefner and I founded our magazines at the same time, fifty years ago in the summer of 1953. Both got going on a shoestring. Hef, by his own account, had less than $200 in the bank—the total investment in *Playboy* was just under $8,000. Our group in Paris had scratched together $1,500 to start *The Paris Review*, a literary magazine. Hef's first issue had the famous calendar shot of Marilyn Monroe. Ours had an interview with E. M. Forster, the great novelist who had not written a novel since 1924. Within months Hef's circulation was in the hundred thousands—an immediate success, "an event waiting to happen," in Hef's words. Our circulation was about three hundred. At its peak *Playboy*'s circulation was seven million; ours crept up to fifteen thousand, which is about all one can hope for with a literary magazine.

Thus it came as a considerable surprise when in the early 1960s A. C. Spectorsky, who was the editorial director of *Playboy*, offered me his job. His great passion, I was to discover, was lounging about on sloops, and though he was relatively young, in his forties, he had it in mind to leave *Playboy* so he could float about on his yacht in the Caribbean and such places.

Why he had me in mind for the job I have no idea. Nonetheless I told him I was greatly flattered. News of the magazine and its flamboyant founder was the talk of the country. I told him it would mean a horrendous change for me—moving to Chicago, giving up a writing career, which I was just beginning, as well as forgoing the editorship of *The Paris Review.* I was single at the time, which was a plus, obviously, but on the other hand there was the problem of informing my mother—not to mention my father, a rather stern Wall Street lawyer—that I had finally found a decent job in Chicago: "And what is that, son?"

One of the pleasures of being offered the job was that it gave me a number of chances to stay at Hefner's Playboy Mansion on North State Parkway. I was fascinated by the place—invariably by the expectation that something was going to happen. The curtains were drawn so that one had the sensation that it was always night. The Centerfold Playmates stayed in the Mansion, and many of the Bunnies who worked at the Playboy Club lived in a kind of dormitory arrangement on the top floor.

On my visits to see Spectorsky I was put in one of the two large rooms on the second floor. One was the Red Room (sometimes called the Rose Room) and the other the Blue Room, each with matching decor. They shared a single bathroom. The Playmate of the Month was invariably in the other room; her toothbrush stood in its glass on the sink. I never could figure out what I would say if our visits to the bathroom coincided.

I remember my friend Jules Feiffer, the cartoonist and dramatist, describing being shown to the Red Room by a butler who then turned and asked Jules if there was anything else he wished.

"When are the girls arriving?" he asked half-jokingly.

Not long after, Feiffer, who had just taken a shower, heard a knock at the door. With a towel wrapped around his middle he opened the door and found himself face-to-face with a lovely long-legged young woman wearing a white blouse and white shorts.

"I had this room before you," she said. "I think I left my radio in here."

"She came in and fetched it," Feiffer said. "And that was the closest I ever came to sex in the Mansion."

The focus of my attention then shifted to the swimming pool in the basement. There was an underwater bar with a large viewing window that looked out on the still, watery depths. A curved stairway led down to the bar. For a more abrupt descent, a trapdoor in the baronial hall above could be raised, and one could slide down a fireman's pole to the floor below. I'd heard, or possibly imagined, that the occasional Playmate—and surely the Bunnies—got carried away and did this.

My favorite haunt was in the pool itself, behind a little waterfall that spilled out over the mouth of a grotto. I would creep in there and stare out through the curtain of water, waiting for something to happen. An hour would pass. I remember the faint smell of chlorine. My skin wrinkled from the chill, and I began thinking of myself as a huge predatory toad as I waited for a Bunny to come down from the dormitory and arc, clothesless, into the pool. If this happened, or if perhaps a dozen girls had plunged in to caper about, throwing a colorful little beach ball around, my plan was to burst through the waterfall, a sudden manic apparition to their startled eyes. This never happened, of course, and after a while I would repair, shivering slightly, to the underwater bar. There I would wait a quiet hour. No one came down the pole or even joined me in the bar. One evening, perched on a stool, I was startled when a tremendous crash, quite audible through the glass, splintered the pool's opaque surface, and a body barely visible in its cocoon of bubbles descended to the bottom of the pool. Almost instantaneously a second body joined the first. Both slowly rose to the surface, and when the bubbles accompanying them dissipated I found that I was looking at two naked, very stout male torsos (their heads remained above the surface) that belonged, I was to discover later, to two comedians. Their legs, pale in the artificial light and as fat as sausages, struggled to keep them afloat. I turned back to my drink.

I never met the comedians. When I went upstairs, they had disappeared like phantoms. Oddly, in my daily rounds of the place I rarely saw anyone. I never met Hef. He was running his empire from the great circular bed somewhere in the Mansion. I wondered if Spectorsky had been in to see him about his new editorial director. At one point, as we lazed about in a calm out on the lake aboard his sloop, he had suggested that he be the editorial director for the first half of the year and I run things for the second; we would alternate until I got the hang of things.

That was my last trip to Chicago. Spectorsky's invitations ceased. Apparently he had found someone else. I was left with my memories of the place. Friends were intensely curious. The Mansion was supposed to be the living embodiment of the magazine. They'd heard that the parties started at one a.m. and went on until dawn. Alex Haley, the novelist, had spoken of once staying in the Mansion and peeking out the slats of a shade to see curious people standing in the street outside and looking at the facade of the building, half expecting, as he put it, that an orgy would tumble out onto the streets.

"Well . . . tell us. What was it like in there?"

I arched an eyebrow. "The Playmate of the Month and I shared a bathroom," I said. "The Bunnies live in the attic." That was all I had to say. They turned away consumed with envy.

When Hef moved the whole shebang to California, it was altogether different. In Chicago it had obviously been bad timing on my part. No doubt parties did go on from one in the morning until dawn, girls with no underwear sliding down the pole into the bar and so forth, but all that kind of merriment had apparently happened on the evenings after I left. On the other hand, the first time I went to the Mansion West I stepped out onto the front lawn to find naked sunbathers, a dozen or so, around the pool; a white llama stepped daintily among them. On the slope beyond: African crowned cranes, peacocks, flamingos. The living embodiment of the magazine indeed! I was particularly taken by the juxtaposition of the sunbathers and the llama, who, alas, eventually died from eating a monogrammed bath towel.

I was there because the photo editor had asked me to try my hand at taking photographs of potential Playmates for the magazine's famous Centerfold. These, along with other candidates, would be shown to Hef, and he would choose what went into the magazine. The photo editor had suggested that I disguise my entries by signing my transparencies with the name Henri Derrière. I thought Henri Derrière as a nom de plume was a bit obvious, and I offered the less suggestive Charles Phillipe.

I took pictures for over a year. I'm rather ashamed to admit that I had a Playboy business card printed with my name and the words *Associate Photographer* underneath. In fact, other than showing it off to friends as a joke, I used the card officially only once. In Tampa, Florida, I brought it out, almost on impulse, and handed it to the receptionist behind the desk at the hotel where I was staying. She was very pretty. She looked at the card and listened to my somewhat stuttered explanation. Would she like to pose? To my astonishment, she agreed. She said, "Oh, well, I'll do it. For a lark!" I rushed out and rented a camera.

When she arrived at my room she shucked out of her clothes as nonchalantly as if stepping out of a bathrobe for a bath. She turned out to have two prominent tattoos, one large butterfly on her rump and a red rose on a hipbone. She said she'd had a "tattoo freak" for a boyfriend and had the tattoos done "for a lark."

"Sometimes they startle people," she said.

I was sure Hef would disapprove of the tattoos (unless they were Playboy Rabbit Head logos), so I asked her to arrange herself in poses that wouldn't show them. We tried props, the hotel Bible from the bedside table, to hide the rose. The results, when I looked at the transparencies, were not encouraging—a pretty girl in strange, awkward postures. In one of them her hand was clutched on her backside as though, at the moment the shutter clicked, she had been hit by a muscle spasm.

Nonetheless I put them away in my portfolio. There were others I'd taken of obliging friends doing it "for a lark."

One friend of mine agreed to pose on the kitchen counter amid an interesting arrangement of pots and pans. Domesticity was the vague concept.

Hef's viewing of potential photographs for the magazine takes place, or did then, in the Mansion's dining room, a portable photo viewer set on the dining room table, plugged in and aglow with opaque light. His photo editors arrived with big manila envelopes, each marked with the name of a potential Playmate and her photographer. I noticed with dismay that one of the envelopes was marked "Henri Derrière." Derrière! My choice of Charles Phillipe had been overruled. It was placed with the others on a Queen Anne sideboard.

It was fascinating to watch Hef at work. He had a brass magnifying eyepiece engraved with his initials and M. WEST for Mansion

West. He moved the eyepiece, a kind of jeweler's loupe, very quickly over the transparencies that had been taken out of the envelopes each in its turn and placed on the viewing panel. He kept up a running commentary, often peppered with somewhat clinical evaluations: "Well, we have a little problem with the fanny here, don't we? It's a cute little problem, though," or "The lips are nice and full, but isn't there a cheekbone problem?" or "I don't think this is the type of girl who lies against satin sheets."

Hef then came across the first of my pictures. He started back from the table as if stunned by what he'd just seen, and a strange sound emerged from his mouth, a kind of strangled cough that I recognized as the laugh of a man overwhelmed with mirth. When he recovered he picked up the slide. "Derrière," he said. "I am not acquainted with his work."

I don't know which slide of mine created such a stir. It might have been the one with the girl lying among the saucepans, perhaps the young woman trying to hide the tattoo on her behind. Whichever, my portfolio was considered inadequate, vastly so, and the photo editor took me aside afterward and said we'd start afresh with a *Playboy* model who knew what she was doing, had no tattoos, and knew enough not to pose among kitchen appliances.

Hef gave me some interesting advice. He told me that a successful, if subtle, ingredient in the early days of the *Playboy* Centerfold had been the unseen presence of a man—a lover, presumably—just out of camera range. The idea of a man being on the premises (his hat on a chair, a pipe on a bedside table) was very much in the *Playboy* tradition. He showed me some examples in *Playboy* back issues—a man's hand coming out of the foreground to offer the Playmate a light for her cigarette, the out-of-focus form of a man (full-length) in evening clothes reflected in a boudoir mirror, who was, in fact, Hefner himself.

He went on to say that the practice had been discontinued. In the moral temper of those times it was thought too suggestive to have pipes and hats, much less the image of a man standing in a bedroom door, accompanying an unclothed Playmate. So that sort of evidence was removed. The girl herself was asked to provide the suggestion in her own mind.

The young woman whom the art department provided me for the Centerfold shot was named Kevyn Taylor—long-legged, slightly freckled, an outdoors kind of girl, not one at her best lying against satin sheets. She was perfectly suited to the scene I had in mind for the photograph, one of a young, unclothed woman standing in a field, having just slipped off a horse. It's been a daydream that has floated about in my mind for years, especially during my callow youth. Even these days, the thought of walking onto a field in autumn, hunting pheasant, a shotgun cradled in my arm, stirs my imagination. Such is the magic of the Playboy organization that the photo editor was able to provide more or less what I had in mind—a meadow of waist-high grass in Topanga Canyon, California. A horse, though, was not provided. The male presence would have to be imagined. I suggested to Kevyn that she imagine that a figure heavily encased in armor had just emerged on a horse from the field's edge.

The Centerfold pictures are taken with an 8" x 10" Deardorff camera—a large boxlike affair that is settled on a thick-legged tripod. It comes with a black sheet that the photographer drapes over the back of his head as he peers through the camera at the focusing screen on which the subject appears. Having taken a crash course in the instrument, I never could get used to the fact that the subject appears upside down on the screen. It was explained to me that a camera works the way the human eye does—the eye transmits an image that is upside down, and the brain makes the proper adjustment. For some reason the Deardorff does not have a compensating mirror to correct the image, so what I saw from under my sheet was Kevyn and the meadow disturbingly upside down. In a way I was relieved not to have the horse of my daydreams standing next to her to add to the topsy-turviness of what I was seeing on the focusing screen. Moreover, the field of focus was so sensitive that at the slightest touch of a knob the tip of Kevyn's nose or the tip of her breast, say, would slide into fuzziness.

It was a sultry afternoon, and I remember an assistant rushing out from time to time with a towel to brush aside a swarm of sweat bees that rose out of the grass and settled around Kevyn's pubic hair.

From under the hood, one picture seemed no better than another. The art department picked the best of them, and it eventually appeared in the magazine—not as a Centerfold, obviously, but in color and interesting enough. It was accompanied by another shot I'd taken of Kevyn in a tree (which pleased me more as an alluring combination of shapes and shadows).

Kevyn told me the night before our shoot that she was fond of hiking and that the best time she'd ever had hiking was walking naked through Big Sur, California, with a girlfriend.

My heart jumped. "Naked?"

"She wore boots and socks. I wore leather shoes."

I asked if anyone had seen the two of them.

She gave me a glance and then said that a couple hiking along the pine trails had spotted them. "The guy looked up and saw me standing there. It must have surprised him."

I grinned and said that without knowing it she had added to the store of my daydreams, that now I had a second sharp image to go along with that of the girl standing in the tall grass next to her horse.

I never thought to ask what Hef thought of Charles Phillipe (a.k.a. Henri Derrière) as a photographer. But I am in his debt for allowing me the chance to try to photograph the Centerfold. When I give a lecture, a hand goes up at the end, and invariably someone wants to know what it's like to photograph a Centerfold. The men lean forward slightly. It is an American daydream.

The daydream for young American women who have the twinge to be an actress or a model always includes the "moment of discovery"—the tap on the shoulder from an agent or a director, very often in the most mundane of circumstances—walking through an airport, in a park, watching a basketball game.

Very late one night when staying at the Mansion West, I came up from the grotto—lurking about among the votive candles—to discover Warren Beatty in the foyer, lying on his back just inside the door, his head resting on a knapsack. He was apparently asleep. I have known Warren for many years. He had been in the Soviet Union, it turned out, to see if he could film parts of *Reds,* his film about John Reed, there, particularly in St. Petersburg, then called Leningrad. The Soviets said he could do so if he agreed to play John Reed in their version of the American Communist's life. Warren had looked at their script, which was patently anti-American, including flash-forwards to the Vietnam War. When Warren turned down the role, the Russians denied him the locales he wanted—the Russian scenes in *Reds* were eventually filmed in Finland. He had returned from these discussions to find that his own house was under such heavy construction repair work that he had come to Hef's, where he knew he could get a night's lodging. I didn't know this at the time—only that he had mysteriously turned up, flat-out on Hef's marble floors. I went up and bent over him. "Warren," I said, "is that you?" His eyes snapped open. "Whigham," he said. "Horace Whigham."

I had no idea what he was talking about. Had he mistaken me for someone else—perfectly understandable, having been aroused from a deep sleep? Apparently not. Horace Whigham was a character in his film, a rather obnoxious, oily magazine editor (could this have been typecasting?) who tries to seduce Louise Bryant, who was played by Diane Keaton. In that split instant—hearing my voice, opening his eyes to find me leaning over him—he had made a casting decision. None of this made any sense to me at the time (Whigham?). Later, of course, he explained what he had in mind, and I eventually ended up playing that small role in a film that won three Academy Awards.

Sometimes when one talks with theater and movie people, their "moment of discovery" (often referred to as "my first big chance") becomes the topic. I can hardly wait to break in.

"Ahem . . . well, I was staying at Hefner's once, and I came walking up from the grotto. . . ."

I have often wondered how I could repay Hef for his hospitality—for the movie nights, the tennis games, the swimming pools, "the moment of discovery," the grotto with the votive candles, the parties and so on. Finally, a few years ago, I got the chance. For another magazine, I had been asked to write about a new French product unknown in this country, most likely even to Hef—a testosterone gel that, when rubbed onto the skin like a salve, was supposed to markedly improve one's libido. What was new about the gel was the place of application. Up until the French salve, testosterone came in a pouch that was most effective when attached to the scrotum, an uncomfortable and cumbersome arrangement. The gel had one alarming side effect, however: If the stuff got on a girl's body during lovemaking, her testosterone level would rise. The chances of masculinization increased—her body fat could redistribute, her voice deepen, her facial hair thicken—all of this quite possible if the lovers were maniacally active. A chemist I talked to gave me a graphic example: "A hair could pop out of her forehead."

To guard against this, the manufacturer suggested that users of the gel wear a T-shirt to keep it from getting on a partner's body. Somehow the notion of Hef slipping out of his dressing gown and getting into a T-shirt did not square with what I had imagined of his lovemaking procedures. Nonetheless, surely he would like to hear about the gel.

I had the chance when I went out to the Los Angeles book fair a few years back. Hef invited me over to watch the championship fight between Michael Grant and Lennox Lewis and to stay around for the disco party afterward. He had separated from his wife Kimberley and was cohabiting with a pair of twenty-two-year-old twin sisters. The twins didn't come down for the fight. Hef sat alone in the darkness on the large couch immediately in front of the large movie screen. I remember a dwarf, an early guest at the party, perched on the far end of the couch. After the fight, which Lewis won easily, Hef gave me a tour of the disco area, a tent on the front lawn.

I mentioned the twins, that I hoped I'd get the chance to meet them.

"Well, we're four now," he said.

"Four! Four of you up there!"

He nodded. He wasn't boasting, just a statement of fact.

"They've imposed a limit," he said. "The girls have. They say that four is enough."

"Hef," I said, "I've been wearing this French testosterone gel. A new product. You rub it on your shoulders."

His eyes widened. To my delight he said he was wearing the testosterone patches. Rather suavely (after all, I was lecturing the man who was the paragon of sexual prowess), I began to describe the gel and how it was applied. I warned him about getting the gel on any of the four, that it was wise to wear a T-shirt. This latter news didn't seem to faze him. His secretary telephoned later in the week. She said that Hef was eager to try the gel.

Last spring during the book fair I dropped in on Hef to pay my respects and to find out how the gel was working. It was the weekly movie night, when Hef puts on old classics for a few of his close friends. He came downstairs in his purple dressing gown. He has not changed over the years—the same wide smile, the warmth of his greeting. I sat next to him at dinner. He told me he was showing *The Citadel* later that evening, the 1938 film starring Robert Donat.

"Hef," I said, "do you remember that French testosterone gel I recommended that you spread on your shoulders?"

He nodded. "I've given it up," he said.

The appalling thought crossed my mind that up there in the great circular bed, two, three, perhaps four of the young women had developed deep voices. . . .

"It had a bad odor," Hef said. "I'm back to the patch."

"Oh."

I asked if any unfortunate symptoms had turned up, if any of the girls had been affected by the gel.

He looked puzzled. He had forgotten about the gel affecting the female testosterone level.

"No excess facial hair?"

"I would have noticed," he said. "Just the odor."

So there it was. Fifty years of association, and I had repaid him for all his kindness by stinking up the great circular bed. But then again, I could comfort myself with the knowledge that it is not all that easy to reward a man who has everything.

Playboy,
JANUARY 2004

Night of the Hunter

—

Hunter called and asked if I would go with him that night to the premiere of *Fear and Loathing* at Loews on 34th. I said I'd meet him at the theater because I had things to do, but he seemed rather agitated—as if a support system to get him through the evening were essential. So I went around to the Carlyle Hotel, where he had installed himself under the curious pseudonym—a kind of oxymoronic alias—Omar Green. The last time he was in New York, he was more direct: Ben Franklin.

Up in his room, other members of his support group were on board: Heidi Opheim, an enchanting, very petite, gamine type who has been with Hunter in Aspen for almost a year; Stacey Hadash, an attractive, blond acquisition-and-merger specialist at Goldman Sachs who has known Hunter since she was introduced to him during the first Clinton campaign by James Carville ("someone asked if I realized I was sitting between two of the weirdest men in America—one [Carville] whose synapses were in overdrive, the other [H.T.] whose synapses were dysfunctional"). Wayne Ewing and his sister Cathy were also on hand. Wayne has been filming Hunter with a video camera for years, intending one day to put together a vast retrospective on the writer's life.

I looked around for Hunter. Apparently he was in the shower. On occasion someone in the room would disappear into the bedroom, eventually relieved by someone else. Everyone seemed to be involved in getting Hunter ready for his premiere, rather like preparing a somewhat balky float for a parade.

I waited in the living room. Stacey mixed me a drink. Traditionally, when Hunter visits New York, she provides him with a number of items from a West Village novelty store she feels will get him through his stay. I had noticed some of them when I entered the room: a severed leg sticking up from behind a sofa cushion, a naked arm on the TV set with its bone sticking out, a dead rat in a trap that twitched convulsively when she flicked a switch on its belly.

"Very lifelike," I said admiringly as it functioned on the carpet.

"We had it in the bathroom last night when Hunter had some friends over to watch the basketball game on television," Stacey said.

I wondered vaguely if the rat would be left behind to startle whomever came in to clean the room when Hunter had gone back to Aspen, or even better, a new hotel guest, sitting down on the bed with a sigh after a long day, and then heading for the bathroom . . . a dying rat in the Carlyle!

There were other totems—two fake knives with retractable blades for kidding around, a small toy ax (equipped with batteries) that when bopped on a hard surface (preferably someone's head), let out a despairing shriek. Last year Stacey provided Hunter with one which, rather than a shriek, emitted the sound of broken glass. At a *Rolling Stone* party at the Lotos Club honoring Hunter, he bopped me with it a number of times. The waitress looked around anxiously, as if glass were underfoot. If you liked him, and it was mutual, it was a kind of benediction to be bopped by Hunter with a toy ax.

Hunter finally emerged from the bedroom. He was wearing a white shirt, a vest, tan trousers, and, of course, the inevitable sneakers. Over the shirt hung a medallion given to him by Oscar Acosta, a lawyer who had accompanied him on the famous trip to Las Vegas that inspired *Fear and Loathing*.

Hunter was ready to leave. There was talk about taking a fire extinguisher with us to the opening. Hunter is very fond of fire extinguishers and operating them in surprising venues, such as a theater. He finally settled on the ax and one of the retractable knives. Other items were checked out: a small pipe, cigarettes, the familiar cigarette holder, and a tumbler of Chivas Regal. On the way out, in the vestibule of the suite, Hunter spotted a single rose in a vase, which he removed and tried to attach to his lapel. Failing this, back in the room over by the sofa where the severed leg stuck out from behind the pillow, he noticed several, tubelike calla lilies in a large vase. These he took, thank goodness, not the leg, and they stayed with us throughout most of the night: four, foot-long stalks that Hunter held out before him like a clutch of spears.

At the theater, photographers on either side of the barricades leaned over as Hunter stepped out of the limousine and led our little cadre full tilt into the street-level lobby. He was booed as he hastened down the red carpet without turning for either microphones or cameras. It was perhaps the booing that precipitated the next complication. Hunter, now happily ensconced in the theater lobby a flight down from the street level, refused to go up to where a phalanx of photographers was waiting to photograph him with Johnny Depp, the star of the picture.

"I'm not going up there," he said, shaking the calla lilies.

The publicity people pleaded with him. I overheard some of it. Apparently the press weren't allowed down on the theater level; Hunter would have to go up.

"They're all waiting up there."

"So what? Why can't they come down?"

"It won't take more than a minute. Johnny Depp's up there."

"I'm not going up. Let them come down here."

I could see the photographers waiting at the top of the stairs, peering down.

"Please, Hunter, just this once."

Finally, as the crowd swirling around us moved into the theater, Hunter agreed to go up to the lobby—but only if the escalator could be reversed so that he could step on it and ride up to the photographers in style.

I heard someone call out, "Where's the escalator button?"

While a search ensued for the button of the escalator, or whatever it was that reversed its direction, Hunter retired to a side room off the lobby and sat down—Achilles to his tent. I sat with him for a moment. I knew Depp was in the theater. I asked about him.

"He came out to Aspen and spent a week. I didn't have to do much. He knows his business. He went down to the basement . . . the sleeping cell."

"I remember that," I said.

"Not many people have been down there," Hunter remarked. "He said he was tortured by brown recluses and black widows."

"That must have fired him up—two species!"

"I think he is a masterpiece in the making."

Back out in the lobby, the photographers suddenly took matters into their own hands. They swarmed down the stairs and backed Johnny Depp against a wall along with Benicio Del Toro, his costar, who plays Dr. Gonzo in the film. Flashbulbs went off. At this point, Hunter emerged from his refuge. He had laid aside his calla lilies and was now carrying an enormous, transparent bag of popcorn. He brushed by me and headed for the photographers. To their delight, he began bopping the actors over the head with his popcorn bag, flailing at them with blows that eventually, of course, broke open the bag, showering everybody within a considerable radius with popcorn. No one seemed at all put out—Hunter, after all, was no longer sulking in his tent but was acting like himself again.

I didn't see much of Hunter during the film, which I enjoyed immensely—Depp's interpretation being uncanny—except to see him striding up the aisle on occasion to have himself a smoke.

A big party was planned afterward at the China Club. The press was waiting, radio teams, television crews. On Hunter's mind was how he was going to watch what was left of the Chicago-Indiana basketball game. Could a television set be provided? The maître d' of the China Club shook his head. Hunter did not take to this kindly. He snapped his calla lilies on the floor like a lion tamer and announced that he was heading for the nearest tavern that had the game on. The publicity people pleaded with him. As we milled about, Wayne Ewing, who had been videotaping the climactic moments of the evening, announced that he'd discovered the club manager had a television set in his office. He'd seen it. So as the guests were coming up the stairs to the party, Hunter headed in the opposite direction for the manager's office. It must have seemed to those arriving that Hunter, hurrying down the stairs, had no use for the party in his honor.

In the office, the two secretaries working at their desks looked up startled as Hunter marched up to a television set that was sitting on a shelf and someone began switching the channels. Hunter let out a sharp yelp of excitement when he got his game and settled on top of a desk to watch.

The manager's office became a kind of VIP room. The word got around upstairs that Hunter was in the building. If you felt you were part of the inner circle, you could find the manager's office and tap on the door. It would then open a crack, speakeasy-style, and if you had the right credentials, you would be let in. Ed Bradley of *60 Minutes*, Jann Wenner of *Rolling Stone*, Walter Isaacson of *Time* magazine, Jimmy Buffett, and Johnny Depp (of course) were among those sitting on the office furniture. Food was brought down. It was very lively in there.

The party upstairs was lively as well. A VIP area. Packed. No Hunter. I spent some time up there. No one seemed to wonder why Hunter wasn't there. Was there some dancing? A band? I think so.

With the game over downstairs, Hunter (disappointed at the Indiana loss) picked up his calla lilies, and we moved on to Jezebel's, a late-night restaurant on the West Side. Things got rather hazy for me after that. A small remnant of the party went on to Elaine's at three in the morning.

It was then, or perhaps later the next day when everything took up again, that Hunter told me this story. It involved throwing a sofa out the window of the 83rd floor of thc Empire State Building—an act brought on by a catatonic rage that had seized a friend of his. Hunter never explained the cause of this man's despair. As this tormented man began wrestling with the sofa, Hunter felt duty-bound to help. A window was opened ("this was back in the days when you could open a window in a skyscraper to do such a thing") and the sofa was jimmied out. The two men had checked to see if the street below was cleared, and it was, blocked off for some reason—a perfect place for the sofa to shatter, no one hurt and no property damage to anything but the sofa itself.

But what happened, according to Hunter, was that on the way down, the sofa took on an aerodynamic lift of its own, caught an updraft, sailed around a corner, and vanished from sight.

"Very surprising," Hunter said. "I mean, we had no idea the sofa was going to do a thing like that . . . go around a corner on us. So we felt we had to get out of there."

"Terrible thing for it to do," I said.

It turned out that the sofa, at the final rush of its descent, had swept through the rear area of what Hunter described as a "Korean food-stall."

"We looked around a corner to see what had happened. There were cantaloupes everywhere. Everyone was running around. They thought an underground explosion had occurred—I mean, something coming out of the sky is not something you'd expect. So their assumption was that something had blown up in the subway system or the gas mains."

"What about the sofa?" I asked.

"They must have figured it was blown up from some janitor's office down there."

I suppose there were some other adventures he told us about at Elaine's, but either I've forgotten or wasn't in a state to remember. I certainly recalled the one about the two men wrestling the sofa out a window of the Empire State Building because I thought, What a wonderful story, an obvious opening for the kind of book Hunter gives us: two men joined in some weird bond very much like that of the two guys barreling into Las Vegas in their red convertible. You learned what had wronged the man who went demented up there, what sort of chemicals were involved, and what had happened after they were down on the street, surveying the wreckage of the Korean food-stall. And as I weaved home on my bicycle not long before the dawn, I thought, Oh, Hunter, write that one, and a lot more . . .

Manhattan File,
1998

The Man Who Was Eaten Alive

—

Twenty years ago, on a beautiful spring day, the English wildlife documentary filmmaker Alan Root came to visit us in Sagaponack, Long Island. He and I took a walk by the ocean with my wife and our daughter, Medora. The tide was up, so the four of us kept close to the dunes. Terns rose on slender white wings and swooped down on us with shrill, reedy cries as they tried to steer us clear of their eggs, which were lying exposed on a sand flat. What was startling was that the terns focused their attention solely on Alan. They careened so close that he threw up an arm as if to ward off an attack.

"They're having a bad day," he probably said, because that was how he often described his difficulties with animals in East Africa—that they were never to be blamed. I don't recall what I said—probably joked and remarked upon his unfortunate karma. I knew that Alan had lost part of his behind during an encounter with a leopard. His right leg had a hole in it from a hippo attack.

The first finger of his right hand was missing. And the middle finger on that hand was a curious twiglike appendage, the result of a puff-adder bite.

That night after dinner, he told us about the hippo attack. The hippo's tusk had gone through his leg, breaking the fibula and leaving a hole that Alan said you could put a "Coke bottle" through—a vivid description that I can still hear him giving, in his soft, almost whispery voice. He showed us the scars, deep holes on either side of his calf.

Since then, I've kept up with whatever Alan happened to be doing. I watched his award-winning nature documentaries on television, among them *Secrets of the African Baobab*, a film about the huge, weirdly shaped trees that the Masai of Kenya believe an angry god pulled up and flung back into the ground upside down; *Mysterious Castles of Clay*, a film about a termite mound and its diverse inhabitants; and *The Year of the Wildebeest*, which traced the huge migrations of the wildebeest herds in the Serengeti. (Alan called it "Brave Gnu World.") His films were among the first to show wild animals in their natural state—without the presence of human spectators. David Attenborough once referred to him as the man who made "natural history filmmaking grow up."

I saw Alan during trips to Africa, and I visited him at his house on Lake Naivasha, where he was living with his first wife, Joan. On one occasion, what I thought was a water bed on the far side of the living room got up, walked out the door, across the grass, and into the lake—a pet hippo named Sally.

Then, a few years ago, I heard that Alan, while shooting a sequence for *Gorillas in the Mist*—a film about the primate expert Dian Fossey, starring Sigourney Weaver—had been charged by a gorilla and injured; a bad shoulder wound was the report. It occurred to me that what Alan truly loved about Africa was slowly chipping away at him: a consortium of hippos, snakes, leopards, and, now, gorillas. I thought that the next time I had the chance I'd pay him a visit and talk to him about how all this had affected his romance with African wildlife.

The chance came last year when I was in Tanzania on a bird-watching expedition. I called Alan, and he suggested that we talk at his new home, near Nairobi, and then fly in his plane down to Mzima Springs, where he had been attacked by the hippo. I was delighted to hear this, though, frankly, I was wary of flying with Alan. He had a bizarre history with airplanes. He told me over the phone that he had recently crashed two helicopters, but that was all right, because he'd ordered a third, from South Africa. I recalled a famous story about Alan's having taken Lord Mountbatten through Hell's Gate, a miniature Grand Canyon in northern Kenya. The plane's wingtips were just yards away from the cliffs on either side, and, at one point, Mountbatten asked, over the roar of the engine, what would happen if someone should be coming the other way. Alan replied that the only other person who flew the gorge was his old friend Iain Douglas-Hamilton, the elephant expert, and it was very simple: if the two were approaching each other head-on, Iain was supposed to go up and Alan was . . . now hold on, Alan was supposed to go up . . . no, wait a minute, Iain . . . and during this palaver Mountbatten sat stiffly, staring straight ahead.

—

Alan and his second wife, Jennie, live on the Athi River, where they have built a dam to form a small water hole. A herd of impalas looked up as I arrived in my taxi. The house, which is of modern design, sits high above the river on an escarpment at the edge of the Nairobi National Park. Alan and I settled ourselves on a terrace overlooking the river. It was good to see him. He looked just the same. The English in Kenya—and especially those who work in the bush for a living—never seem to change. Alan, who stands slightly over six feet, has tousled sandy-graying hair, which seems to have rarely had a brush or a comb put to it; a face permanently reddened by the sun; round glasses that give him a slightly owlish look; and that soft voice, which seems so at odds with the adventurous life he's led. Now in his sixties, fit and trim, he hardly seems the worse for the peculiar kind of wear he's been through.

Jennie brought out some tea. She is ill with leukemia—very thin, pale. The fact that she has survived the disease for sixteen years is undoubtedly due, in part, to the intensely compassionate relationship between the two of them. Alan once wrote me, "I have learned so much from this wonderful woman, and it is so hard to see her betrayed by her body." She sat with us for a while, laughing softly from time to time when Alan touched on something that amused her. He began, at my request, to talk a bit about himself. Born in England, in 1937, he had come out to Kenya ten years later, from London's war-torn East End, when his father took a job as the plant manager of a meat-packing factory twenty-odd miles southeast of Nairobi. There was wildlife everywhere—it was a time when leopards were a common enough sighting in the suburbs—and Alan was infatuated with it. At school, he put on an exhibit called Root's Reptiles. "My parents knew nothing about wildlife, but they were happy to let me do anything I wanted to do, though they didn't want me to keep poisonous snakes," he said. "In fact, I had snakes all over the house, in pens and pits—cobras, puff adders. I just told my parents that they weren't poisonous. My poor old mom didn't know the difference—this great, bloody puff adder in a crate in a corner of the room. She thought it was harmless until the day she died."

In 1952, the Mau Mau insurrection erupted in Kenya, and a state of emergency was declared that lasted for seven years. Alan was released from school—which he disliked intensely—and he spent a couple of years "chasing the Mau Mau," as he put it, around the forests of the Aberdare Mountains. Many of his compatriots went on to become professional big-game hunters, putting to practice what they had learned while tracking the Mau Mau. Alan, on the other hand, used his expertise to further the interest he'd shown with Root's Reptiles—capturing animals for the world's zoos. Exploring the Aberdares and their bamboo forests, he learned how to capture the rare bongo antelope, an animal so highly strung that it invariably dies from shock if mishandled. When Alan started the project, there were almost no bongos in captivity. Within five years, he captured nearly thirty of them. Since they breed easily—"like flies"—he shut down his camp. "I caught all the bongos the world needed," he said at the time.

Over the years, Alan has kept a number of pets, many of which were brought to him as orphans: cheetahs, leopards, waterbucks—everything, he said, except a giraffe. I asked which species had been the most difficult to raise. He picked the aardvark—the insect-eater that has a snout almost as long as the rest of its body. "Very difficult animal," Alan said. "It needs termites. It came to us as an orphan when Joan and I were living on Lake Naivasha. We took on the cook's son to look after the aardvark. The boy was retarded, and could never get any work. It was a wonderful arrangement. All he had to do was follow the aardvark around. It would dig these enormous holes. The cook's son would fill them in. Then the aardvark would move on and dig another huge hole, dig himself completely out of sight, and the cook's son would wait for him to climb out."

"You name your pets," I said. "What did you call the aardvark?"

"Million," Alan replied.

"Million?"

"Yes, as in 'Aardvark a million miles for one of your smiles.' "

"Oh, yes."

I asked him about the pet hippo I'd mistaken for a water bed.

"Sally," Alan said. "Her mother died in the 1974 drought, at Lake Baringo. Sally was about the same size as the aardvark. They would walk around together. So the cook's son had double responsibility. Sally loved sucking on pillows. Security blankets. With her chin on the edge of the sofa, she'd suck these things. After a while, they weren't much to look at—or to sit on for that matter."

We began talking about Alan's early career as a filmmaker. During the years he spent trapping animals, Alan had also made an eight-millimeter film, more or less of home-movie quality, which had come to the attention of an East African Airways pilot and would-be film producer. He hired Alan to shoot the day-to-day activities of a bird called a lily-trotter, a curious long-legged waterfowl with extra-long toes that enable it to walk on water-lily leaves. The film led to Alan's next job, which was to photograph animals in the Serengeti for a popular British series entitled *On Safari.* In the Serengeti, Alan met Bernhard Grzimek, a zoologist from Frankfurt, Germany, who was planning a documentary about the movements of the wildebeest and the zebra.

"Grzimek got me involved in a strange scientific experiment," Alan recalled. "He had been a veterinarian in the war. Not much to do—very few horses—so he began experiments on animal recognition to determine the visual requirements necessary for an animal to identify another member of its species. Would a real horse nuzzle up to a fake one—a Cubist horse, for example?"

"Not much help to the German war effort," I said.

"Very little," Alan agreed. "And I'm sure Grzimek was happy

about that. But he was obsessed with what he was doing, and he carried on his experiments in East Africa. A toymaker in Germany made these inflatable rubber animal dolls—pretty grotesque—to see what wild animals in the Serengeti would make of them.

"Predictably, the animals we'd thought were going to be smart turned out that way," Alan went on. "Elephants—they either ran away or made demonstration charges. Others weren't smart at all. The rhinos! I would walk toward them holding this huge fake rhino by the hind legs, and the rhinos would come up and head-butt, carrying on as if they were the best of friends with this thing. One day, we came across a female rhino, very aggressive. Not only did she have a calf but she was also in season. Males had come around; she had chased away a couple of them. I came up to her with my rubber rhino. She went for it and tore it open with her horn. It immediately deflated—phffft. I had felt very safe behind the thing, and suddenly it was gone! There I was, standing right in front of her, ten feet away, and watching her go absolutely bananas. The fake rhino swirled around in the air like a balloon let loose, and the remains of it landed on the real rhino's back. Fortunately, she thought that something had jumped on her, so she whirled around. By the time she had turned in my direction, I'd made it safely to the car."

Alan said that, although he admired Grzimek's strong views on conservation, he disagreed with him about whether human beings should be photographed with the animals, for dramatic purposes. In those days, a typical device was to show the animals being viewed by tourists on safari; invariably, one of the tourists was a young woman in jodhpurs and safari hat, who would exclaim in delight at sighting a baboon family. Alan felt strongly that animals could carry the show on their own. His opinions were dismissed not only by Grzimek but also by the home office in Frankfurt, which kept sending cables: "This new batch of films was great. The elephants were a bit out of focus. We're still waiting for the naked women."

One day, Grzimek asked Alan to round up a group of Masai girls. "They'll be bathing," Grzimek said. "Naked. Splashing water on each other. An animal on the side of the pool will frighten them and they'll all run out, dripping."

"I'd grown up in this very uptight community, and it wasn't easy for me," Alan recalled. "But in the end we found eight good-looking girls—not Masai but from Nairobi. They were suitably buxom, and we put them in this pool, splashing around, and then we made a noise that was supposed to be an angry wild animal, and they all rushed out of the pond and into a grove of fever trees. Then a shot of a leopard filmed many miles away in a fever tree was cut in. . . . Innocent days. The film was called *Serengeti Shall Not Die*. Got an Oscar the next year."

Alan continued, "The amazing thing about Grzimek was how he would ruin his wonderful nature films by introducing the human stuff. The film would have this great footage of a lion charging a wildebeest, and then suddenly you'd be watching a veterinarian in the zoo removing a golf ball from a cheetah's mouth."

—

In 1962, when Alan was twenty-six, he was given the opportunity to make the kind of films he wanted to do. A small British production company had recently made a highly praised documentary about the animals of London's Hyde Park—mainly squirrels and swans. Its managing director, Aubrey Buxton, decided that his cameras should venture farther afield. He traveled to East Africa in search of Alan, whose work he had admired, and found him on the far bank of the Rutshuru River, in the Congo. The river was in its flood stage, so Buxton had to shout his offer—for Alan to make a series of nature films—across a tumult of water. Alan accepted, and he has been with Survival Anglia—as Buxton's company came to be called—ever since.

Alan went on to tell me about what was perhaps the most peculiar project he did for Survival Anglia—the documentary-length survey of a termite mound, entitled *Mysterious Castles of Clay.*

"Not an easy subject to sell," I suggested.

Alan nodded. "Survival needed to sell the film in the States, and the distributors got very concerned," he said. "The head honcho said, 'Around here, "termites" is the same kind of word as "cancer." Ninety percent of Americans have homes built of wood. They don't want to hear about termites.' So I went off and made it anyway." Alan's termite film turned out to be one of the most honored nature films ever made, winning both a Peabody and an Oscar nomination.

I asked him about a memorable moment in a short film he had made about the shooting of *Mysterious Castles of Clay*. In the scene, his wife Joan had enticed a spitting cobra to let loose a stream of venom with such accuracy that the poison hit the protective mask she was wearing. This got us to talking about snakes, which led to my inquiring about the puff-adder bite that had destroyed most of the first and middle fingers of Alan's right hand.

The accident occurred in 1968, in Joy Adamson's camp in the Meru National Park, in Kenya. Along with Joan, Alan had flown there with an American in the movie business who wanted Adamson—the celebrated author of *Born Free*, about Elsa, her pet lioness—to lend her name to a 3-D project involving animals. "I went off for a walk around camp," Alan recalled, "and I found this huge puff adder—a female, really big and fat, four and a half feet long, which is large for the species. Puff adders are quite easy to catch. Their heads are arrow-shaped, and you can get them by the neck. I thought that Adamson's visitor would be interested in seeing one, so I brought it into camp. I showed him how the fangs worked, lifting them out of their recesses with a knife edge. Joy brought out her camera and took some pictures. Then I put the snake down to let it sidle off into the bush. Just then, Joy announced that she didn't have any film in her camera. So I went after the puff adder and tried to catch it the same way. It was waiting for me, and it struck, getting me on the knuckle. Excruciating pain—right from the start. The problem was that I'd been bitten a few years earlier by a burrowing viper, which isn't fatal but is quite painful, and, as a cure, I'd been given an antivenom. The next time you take an antivenom, the body will fight back and you can get a shock reaction, so I decided not to have it. Halfway on the flight to Nairobi, I started vomiting—fainting, dizziness, and so on. I decided I'd better have the antivenom. Joan gave me three ccs of the stuff in the muscle. By the time we got to the hospital, I couldn't walk. I was rushed inside, and the people there obviously thought I was in this terrible state because of the snakebite, when in fact I was having an allergic reaction to the antivenom. Joan was outside paying the taxi driver. Before she could come in and explain, they gave me another ten ccs—this time intravenously. I went into anaphylactic shock. They rushed me to the emergency room, where I was resuscitated. Then the puff-adder poison took over. It works slowly. After two or three days, my whole right arm went completely black. It looked like a row of black plums, huge blisters full of blood that ran all the way down from my armpit to my waist. In the end, it was necessary to amputate only the first finger."

After getting out of the hospital, Alan had dinner with Richard Leakey, who was then the director of the National Museums of Kenya. He presented Leakey with the remains of his finger in a covered dish. "I told him that it was the first installment of bits bitten off, the rest to follow in various jars."

I laughed and said, "You had a premonition that more was to come."

Alan smiled. I leaned forward and said, "I'm surprised that you let the puff adder go. Dangerous to have around camp."

"The puff adder was having a bad day," he said. "Not its fault at all."

"How about that leopard? Do you bear it any ill will for what it did to you?"

Alan said, "Three of us had been filming all morning in the Serengeti. We walked up one of those boulderlike hills—what are called kopjes—clapping our hands and making noise in case there was something sleeping or hiding in the bushes. Nothing. So we went to the top of the kopje and had a nice lunch. I saw an owl fly out from an overhanging rock. We figured that something must have disturbed it, so we climbed to the top of the rock and looked down and we saw a dead jackal lying there—freshly dead, not a mark on him. I'd had a beer for lunch, and I wasn't really thinking very clearly, because obviously a dead jackal doesn't frighten an owl. I decided to jump down—a six-foot drop—and investigate. Well, right underneath the overhang of the rock was a leopard. He'd heard us talking, just above him. I landed with my knees bent and my backside straight in the leopard's face. He jumped out"—Alan made a guttural roar as illustration—"and bit me twice in the buttocks, and then ran off down the slope. The bites didn't hurt at all—not a lot of nerve endings there—but the wounds were deep, and there was a spectacular amount of bleeding, pouring down my legs. I thought I'd better report to the warden of the Serengeti, my friend Myles Turner. I walked into his office, squirting blood. He could see I wasn't badly hurt. He said, 'What happened to you?' I said, 'One of your leopards has bitten me in the bum.' He looked at me and said, 'You know you're not allowed to feed animals in the park. Get out of here!' "

—

The next day, Alan and I flew down from Nairobi to Mzima. Our flight was reasonably uneventful—at least, by his standards. As we neared Mzima, the flat country gave way to rolling hills. Alan said that we were over the country of the Wakamba, the great hunters of the Serengeti. He pointed out, high on the grass slopes, a small herd of eland that appeared to be pursued and then caught and passed by the plane's shadow. The hill country gave way to ancient, quiescent volcanoes, pocket-size and quite close to one another. From above, they looked like barnacles on a waterlogged piece of timber. The ash from the volcanoes provides a natural water filter for the Mzima Springs, a series of ponds, like a vast aquarium, which allow a crystal-clear view of whatever is moving around within—fish, turtles, the spotted-necked otter, crocodiles, hippos. That afternoon, Alan showed me the pool where his disastrous encounter with the hippo had occurred. We could see the backs of four or five hippos above the water level—motionless, hardly alarming.

"I was filming while wearing an Aqua Lung," he said. "Upstream, two males started to scrap—nothing to do with me—running half in and half out of the water, and it stirred up all this mud and hippo dung on the bottom, so that there was zero visibility. We had a guy filming me and my wife—filming us making a film. I had told everyone not to swim around if the water got stirred up but to stay still, sit on the bottom, and the current flow would clear everything in a few minutes. So we were all sitting on the bottom, pretty nervous. Because we weren't sure where these hippos were, we were breathing heavily. Lots of bubbles. And one of the hippos—I think the one who lost the fight—came back, and, seeing all those bubbles on the surface, thought they came from the hippo he'd been fighting, so he charged into the bubbles, slashing with his jaws. One of his tusks caught Joan's face mask and shredded the rubber and broke the glass—incredibly, without touching her skin. She had no idea what had happened—just that her face mask had suddenly vanished. The hippo turned, and I felt the pressure of the wave. It knocked me backward, and my legs came up in the air. He caught them in his mouth and shook me like a dog with a slipper. The people on the bank said that I came up out of the water three times, and then went back down. The hippo kept banging me on the bottom. And then, suddenly, he stormed off. I can remember very vividly hearing the sound of the tusks scissoring my legs, and I could feel the whiskers of his chin on the back of my thighs. My cameraman saw all the blood and pulled me up onto the bank. The tusk broke the smaller of the two bones in the leg, and it left a hole"—I knew what was coming—"that you could put a Coke bottle through. I got in the back of the car with a bottle of Glenfiddich and off we went to the airstrip. A bit of gangrene set in, but they fixed it at the hospital in Nairobi. Then, after two months, we went back to Mzima and finished up."

"Could you recognize the hippo that got you and shook you the way a dog shakes a slipper?"

"Oh, yes," Alan said. "A low-ranking male. He'd obviously been beaten up a lot. Many scars. I'm sure that he meant no malice toward me."

Once again, I was struck by Alan's compassion for animal life, despite the deprivations he had endured. He once told the writer and filmmaker John Heminway that upon his death he wanted to be laid out on the Serengeti—his remains to be eaten by vultures, hyenas, beetles, and botflies, as a way of repaying his debt to wildlife. I mentioned this, and Alan said, "We'll have to find a secluded place. There are so many tourists with video cameras these days. I wouldn't want shots of vultures fighting over my extremities to end up on CNN."

I laughed and said, "Yes, you wouldn't want to have people saying, 'That fellow's having a bad day.' "

We spent that night in a tent compound a few hundred yards from the Mzima Springs, as guests of two filmmakers, Victoria Stone and Mark Deeble. They were engaged in very much the same kind of work—with vastly superior equipment—that Alan had done many years earlier.

The evening was cool. We ate outside. Mark put a Coleman lamp on the table, its wick set low, so that the faces of our little group were barely discernible at the edge of the darkness. A bottle of whiskey was produced. East Africa gossip. I was basking in the pleasure of where I was when I heard Mark say, "Peter Jenkins, who was the warden at Ithumba, was driving along under an escarpment near Voi when a rhino fell out of the sky and landed with a great crash just in front of him."

"Yes," Alan said. "I've heard that."

Mark went on, "Rhinos get to chasing each other around up there near the edge of the escarpment, and, since they don't see at all well, one of them will go off the edge."

We sat in the darkness and contemplated the spectacle of a falling rhino and the sound of it fetching up against the road. I said that I was reminded of a story I'd once heard—that some passengers on the bridge of a Dutch freighter pumping along in the Indian Ocean had suddenly been alarmed by two tremendous splashes a hundred yards or so off the bow, one after the other. When the ship slowed down, they discovered two dead cows floating with their legs up.

"Hmm."

I went on to explain that a Russian cargo plane carrying a shipment of cattle from Argentina to Minsk, or some such place, had found itself in trouble over the Indian Ocean when the cows started bellowing and stampeding back and forth. The only solution was to lower the back cargo door and get rid of some of the more obstreperous animals.

"Hmm."

I said, "Your rhinos dropping into the road reminded me of it."

"Hmm."

This was typical of storytelling in Africa: there seemed never to be much of a reaction, even a cluck of astonishment or a request for amplification ("Why just two cows?"). After a while, you got used to it—letting the story run clean. I liked to think, of course, that the story was being filed away for future use—that Mark, say, would clear his throat at the fireside a year hence and begin, "This American chap was telling about this Russian cargo plane. . . ."

Alan finally broke the silence. He said, "I like the sound of hippos munching grass."

We began talking about noises in the African night. Alan said that the loudest unexpected sound he'd ever heard at night had erupted from a friend, Ian Parker, who was out by the latrine beyond the edge of a clearing. Pulling up his trousers, he had been bitten in the rear by a very large scorpion. "A great bellow," Alan said.

Back in Nairobi, I finally heard the full story about Alan's mishap during the filming of *Gorillas in the Mist*. "My job was to film a gorilla charge for the scene where Dian Fossey meets the gorillas," Alan told me. "I took the job because it kind of closed the circle for me. I had shown Fossey her first gorilla. It's hard to find a gorilla that charges all the way. Most of them are so accustomed to people watching them that it's very hard to get them to do very much. But there was a gorilla that everyone had heard about in the Kahuzi area, in Zaire. Very bad-tempered. His father had been killed by a poacher. He had killed a poacher."

"A lone gorilla? A rogue?"

"No, he had a family, but he was a dangerous animal. We

found them the first day. I was wearing a big body mount to hold the camera, and I had to stand up with the camera fixed at eye level. I said to my assistant that it was crazy—the worst sort of body language to show a gorilla, because it looked like a weapon. We had found their tracks and were sitting there having coffee. I decided to attach a telephoto lens rather than get too close to him. While I was doing this, a younger male came up to take a look at us. He eventually got quite curious, and he began working his way toward us until he was only twenty yards or so away. When we stood up to film the older males, the young male didn't want to move. He sat there, watching us get closer and closer. I kept saying to him, 'Get going! Go on with you!' Then, suddenly, he panicked. He leaped up and ran, making a nervous, grunting sound. The big male—we couldn't see him—obviously heard him. He must have assumed that someone was chasing his kids: 'Got to do something about this!' "

Alan continued, "When a gorilla charges, basically it's just bluff: he tries to make himself as big as possible; he rears up, spreads his chest, and it's all to impress you. But this was completely different—no bluff at all. He came around the corner like a fucking great Doberman, low to the ground, looking straight at me. I started filming. He went out of focus almost immediately, and the next thing I knew he was on me. He grabbed me like a man grabbing a turkey—by the waist and one leg. He bit me on the leg and threw me down—teaching me a lesson—and then he ran off. Since I'd fallen backward, with the camera strapped to me, I couldn't get up. I thought he'd gutted me. He'd grabbed me by the waist with those huge hands—I'm sort of ticklish anyway—but the bite was actually in my thigh."

Alan showed me the scar: a U-shaped curve on his leg just above the knee. It looked as though a large slab of flesh had been lifted up and then settled back in place. He said, "I had a few weeks in hospital in Nairobi." I wondered whether the people in the hospital were getting accustomed to these visits of his: "Ah, here we are again. What was it this time?"

After he got out of the hospital, Alan returned to the movie set. "I went back to the same gorilla," he said. "He was the only one who would give us what we wanted. We approached him differently, though—he was still very belligerent. We got the charging scenes, but this time he didn't have a good reason to come all the way at me."

I said, "That's quite something, going back to him."

"He was having a bad day that last time—a combination of the wrong body language with that equipment and the situation with the young male." Alan paused and grinned. "If you think his charge was impressive, you should have seen the bill I put in to Warners!"

While I was getting ready to leave for the Nairobi airport, I said to Alan, "Have we covered everything? Hippo, leopard, puff adder, gorilla—anything else?"

"Well," Alan said, "I was once stabbed by a duiker—a little male antelope. Fierce little guys. They have very sharp horns that make neat punctures that close up and then turn septic. It was, in fact, my sister's duiker, and that made it worse."

"Hmm."

"I suppose I should show you this," he said. He pointed to a thin diagonal scar on his upper lip.

"What did it?" I asked.

"I was bitten by my pet mongoose."

I knew what he was going to say next, and he did:

"He was having a bad day."

The New Yorker,
AUGUST 23, 1999

I Played the Apollo

—

Almost all the newspapers in their Ella Fitzgerald obituaries last June noted that the singer's career had started at the age of sixteen, when, for singing "The Object of My Affection," she won first prize—twenty-five dollars—while competing on Amateur Night at Harlem's Apollo Theater. The Apollo's Amateur Night is a Wednesday-evening tradition that continues to this day.

Back in the sixties, I went up to 125th Street to Amateur Night quite often, not so much in the hope of being in on the discovery of a great talent as to enjoy being part of what was essentially a kind of "happening," and to admire those who were courageous enough to risk the most extreme forms of derision. One afternoon, I called the authorities there and asked if I could compete in the contest.

"Doing what?"

I said that I was an odd kind of reporter, a "participatory journalist," and I wanted to perform a short piano piece of my own composition on Amateur Night in order to write about the experience. Somewhat puzzled, the Apollo's impresarios agreed.

In the weeks before my scheduled appearance, I became a regular on Wednesday night, and I picked up quite a bit of lore. The traditions of Amateur Night at the Apollo are time-honored. First of all, emerging from stage left, the contestant touches the shellacked stump of a tree set on an Ionic column. "The Tree of Hope" it is called. The original tree—a chestnut—shaded the backstage alley between the Lafayette Theatre and Connie's Inn, on Seventh Avenue at 132nd Street. For years, it was a kind of Rialto for performers: they sat around its base and gossiped—in such numbers that when an agent was looking for an act it was just a question of dropping by the tree to see who was available. When it was cut down, in 1933, during the widening of Seventh Avenue, a piece was retrieved for the Apollo. Some contestants spend a lot of time at the tree, rubbing the smooth sheen of its surface as if spreading out the wrinkles in a bedsheet—on the chance that some vague osmotic relationship will link them with predecessors who have touched the Tree of Hope and gone on to become stars.

Next, after being introduced to the audience by the master of ceremonies, the contestant launches into a song, a dance, a juggling act—whatever. The success or failure of the effort depends upon the reaction of the audience, which functions as judge, very much as the crowds in Rome's Colosseum determined whether the gladiator would get a thumbs-up or a thumbs-down from the emperor's box. Sometimes the audience is divided in its opinion, and the contestant must strive to continue through a buffeting of boos and cheers until one side or the other prevails. If the contestant is successful, he or she appears in a lineup at the end of the show. Once again, the audience applauds, and the top four applause-getters move on to the monthly Show-Off. A contestant who continues to win will eventually reach the quarterly Top Dog Show-Off, which, as one would imagine, is attended by talent scouts. Stardom may not follow—although, besides Fitzgerald, the event has helped launch, among many others, Billie Holiday, Nina Simone, James Brown, the Ink Spots, the Coasters, Gladys Knight and the Pips, and the Jackson Five (Michael was ten at the time)—but, even when it doesn't, the contestant has been through quite an experience. The usual Broadway tryout pales by comparison.

If the contestant is unsuccessful, and the chorus of boos and whistles overwhelms the cheers, a fire siren goes off backstage, and a human representation of the "hook" appears, outlandishly dressed and often firing a pistol or brandishing a broom or a baseball bat; after capering about in a wild dance, he escorts the contestant backstage.

At the Apollo, the human hooks are referred to as Executioners. Over the years, there have been several Executioners. The first, back in the thirties, was Norman Miller—a short, foul-mouthed, potbellied stagehand called Porto Rico. He came onstage in a number of guises: a farmer with a shotgun, an old woman with a broom, the Old Man of the Mountain, a hermit with a pitchfork, or—the noisiest of them—a grinning lunatic wearing a homemade suit of pots and pans. He was followed, after the war, by a man called the Great Adam. He was waiting in the wings the night I performed: a thin-shanked kid, who was, as I recall it, a bootblack at the time. Like his predecessor, he had fashioned a number of costumes for himself, among them a Batman outfit. One night as the Great Adam was prancing about the stage in this costume, a contestant hauled off and socked him. The Great Adam toppled over in a heap, flat out, and the stagehands had to rush on and remove the contestant, his feet kicking as they lifted him up and hurried him away. The night I performed, the Great Adam wore a pair of long johns and carried a small cap pistol.

He was succeeded by Howard "Sandman" Sims, who became one of the Apollo's famous characters. Before he became the Executioner, the Sandman sat up in a box overlooking a corner of the stage. As I remember him sitting there, he was outfitted in a shabby clown costume, over which he wore a string of Christmas-tree lights. He played—or, rather, *had*—a trombone, and when he disapproved of the performer on the stage below he would raise it to his lips and blow a swooping, sirenlike blast to signal to the Executioner that it was time for him to make an appearance. (In his early days, the Sandman would swing down on a rope from his box to the stage and do the job himself.) He was called Sandman because when he first came to New York, as a teenager, from North Carolina, he used to sprinkle a patch of sand on a sidewalk and dance across it, creating a scratching sound, like brushstrokes on a drum, and there was no one who could do it the way he did. Or, as he described it, "They ain't nobody who can whips they's feet like I can."

—

The present Executioner is C. P.—for "Crowd Pleaser"—Lacey, who has been on the job since one night in 1986, when he substituted for Sandman Sims, who had taken a leave of absence to play a part in the film *Tap*. Lacey, whose given name is actually Carlos Preston, was originally a street performer, setting a cloth hat out on the sidewalk and attracting an audience with gyrating dances in imitation of, among others, Elvis Presley, James Brown, Michael Jackson, and Tina Turner. (He doesn't like doing Turner, he says, because women's high heels hurt his feet.) These days, he is billed as America's Premier Comic Impressionist. The James Brown split is his specialty. Often, at the end of Wednesday evening, he sings "Please, Please, Please," complete with jumps and splits. "I learned the split the hard way," he told me not long ago. "After about killing myself, I bought the James Brown video and learned off that." He paused, then said solemnly, "I strongly recommend that you get the James Brown tape before you try the James Brown split."

"I'm very glad to hear this," I said, as if the James Brown split—actually a kind of half split preceded by a great leap—was the first thing I had in mind to do when I got home.

C.P., like his predecessors, has a number of Executioner costumes. When I met him, he was sporting three ties, an oversized coat, and a multicolored wig.

Cruel as these Executioners must seem to the contestants, it struck me that the hook is a compassionate procedure—at least, as utilized at the Apollo—in that the audience's attention is instantly removed from the hapless contestant and focused on the Great Adam, say, lunatic in his big Dr. Dentons, as he capers around the stage, his little cap pistol popping. Indeed, the contestant can escape to the sanctuary of the wings in a storm of applause which, though it's not meant for him, is surely more comforting than a crestfallen exit to a chorus of catcalls.

The Executioner is not the only presence to reckon with on Amateur Night. Roaming the house there used to be a person known as the Geech, who, dressed in women's clothes, went up and down the aisles plaintively and loudly calling for someone named Richard: "Rich . . . *ard!*"

Another formidable personage is Eva Isaac (also known as Miss Apollo), who has a regular seat in the front row, which she has now occupied on Amateur Night for almost forty years. She is very quick to act as an orchestra-level Executioner, shooing off failed performers with violent hand motions. A great fan of Al Green, and also of Otis Redding and Sam Cooke, she is a harsh critic of any contestant who tries to imitate these famous singers, and it is considered wise to leave their work out of one's repertoire. Often, if she particularly likes an act—especially that of a male singer—she climbs onto the stage and does a somewhat tipsy dance around the contestant, now and then stroking him like a large pet. The fact that Eva is on the stage is of considerable comfort to performers, because as goes Eva so goes the house. On the other hand, to negotiate and reach the high notes of a finale, say, cannot be easy with Eva draped around one's person like a boa.

And then there is the audience itself. It packs the house—all fourteen hundred and seventy seats—on Amateur Night. It is raucous, enthusiastic, and keenly judgmental. Even the master of ceremonies' standard question to his audience—"Having a good time?"—gets a smattering of "No!'s." Traditionally, he reminds his listeners of their responsibilities ("If you think the contestants need a little woodshedding, let 'em know. Let 'em know if tonight is not their night."), and his listeners certainly take the reminder to heart. The quickest hook I've heard of was administered to a white man who came onstage to sing "Pardon My Southern Accent" and was booed off before he was able to get out a single note. Another quick decision involved an enormously fat man, well over four hundred pounds, who walked briskly across the stage and then stopped abruptly, his flesh quivering like a sharply struck hillock of Jell-O. That was all he did, and it didn't go over well with the people out front: they immediately called for the Executioner.

And yet the audience can be compassionate. One story I treasure is about an amateur who was singing so badly that, before the Executioner could get to him, a stagehand flipped the switch controlling the microphone, sending it down into a recess below the stage. As it slowly descended, the singer followed it, until finally he was on his knees, still singing, with his head just off the floor. The audience, admiring his determination, quieted down and then began cheering as the microphone began its rise; the singer got up off his knees, and eventually stood upright, his rendition still full of dreadful wrong notes but now delivered to a standing ovation.

It was into this cauldron that I ventured. At home, I had been spending a couple of hours a day at the piano. I am not very serious about the piano. I know only three or four pieces—among them "Tea for Two" and "Deep Purple"—but I enjoy improvising, and the result is music that one of my friends has described as sounding like the background music on the soap opera *The Edge of Night*.

The Wednesday I was to perform, I left a cocktail party and arrived at the Apollo in a dark business suit and a somber tie. The night's program was devoted almost entirely to rock-and-roll acts. We gathered in what was then called the Dungeon—a basement room containing a dozen broken-down theater seats, their stuffing showing, a table, a number of music stands, and, above a door, a mysterious red-lettered cardboard sign that read "All Those Who Enter Here," the rest of it torn away. Through this dank room moved a shifting, restless crowd of would-be performers, self-absorbed, mute, and utterly miserable. All my fellow contestants were black. One of them was a young girl—around ten, I would guess—wearing tap-dancing shoes that clickety-clicked as she walked nervously among us. I suppose if anyone had looked at me, in my business suit and tie, they might have assumed that I was an important talent scout. There were no introductions.

The master of ceremonies at that time was Honi Coles: a slim, elegant dancer, he was a partner in the famous tap-dancing team of Coles & Atkins. Listening at the bottom of a curved iron staircase leading to the stage level, we could hear him joshing with the crowd. The Great Adam walked through the Dungeon in his union-suit outfit. We all stared at him.

I stood in the wings to watch the act immediately preceding mine. The contestant was playing an old-fashioned watering can. I had only a glimpse of how he was playing the thing—blowing across the mouth of the spout and, with his free hand, lifting its lid and setting it down again, as if it were a jazz drummer's high-hat cymbal. I wish I could remember the sound he produced; I suppose it was something rather like the hoot you get when you blow across the neck of a large bottle. In any case, the audience took umbrage and called for the Great Adam to move him out of sight. I recall thinking that anyone who could get *any* sound out of a watering can, much less a vaguely recognizable tune, should be allowed to hang in there, if only for the novelty. Instead, with the Great Adam behind him, he came off the stage murmuring, and cradling his curious instrument to his chest as if he were carrying a Stradivarius.

It was my turn. I was firmly convinced that I would last only a few minutes. The first whistles would start, and, not long afterward, the bray from the Sandman, in his box, would bring out the Great Adam to escort me back into the wings. I told the Great Adam as much: "It won't be long."

I stepped out onto the stage. I touched the Tree of Hope.

Honi Coles was waiting to meet me. He asked my name and where I lived. It helps if you come from Manhattan (as I do), because most of the audience comes from Harlem. There was a certain amount of encouraging clapping.

"What are you going to play?" Coles asked.

I said, "I'm going to play the piano."

His eyebrows rose slightly. He spoke with studied affectation: "And what is the name of the musical composition with which you are intending to entertain us, if I may ask?"

The fact is that I had not named the work. It tended to change every time I played it, as if I were poking at a piece of quicksilver.

"I guess it's Opus No. 1," I said.

"Opus No. 1," he announced to the audience.

I walked over to the piano. I remember how foreign the keyboard looked, and how consciously I had to figure out where to arrange my fingers for the opening chords.

I began. Over the vapid sounds of Opus No. 1, I could hear the audience beginning to make up its mind—first a few whistles, which usually precede the booing. I was conscious of the Sandman up behind me, leaning over the railing of his box, and I suppose I must have hunched my shoulders slightly, cringing, waiting for the blat of his trombone. But nothing. A few handclaps. No reaction from Miss Apollo, Eva—probably because what I was playing bore very little resemblance to Al Green, Otis Redding, or Sam Cooke.

I began to realize that I had a chance—a slight chance—of getting through the piece.

So I finished Opus No. 1. I caught a glimpse of the Great Adam standing in the wings. He grinned and gave me a thumbs-up sign. I stood and bowed—rather awkwardly, as if someone were pushing me in the back.

In the lineup at the end of the show, my performance won second prize. The young tap dancer, who had sung "Dancing Shoes" as she clickety-clicked across the stage, won first prize. Jack Schiffman—the son of Frank Schiffman, who took over the Apollo with a partner, in 1935—writes in his book *Uptown: The Story of Harlem's Apollo Theatre,* that I "treated the startled audience to a tasteful rendition of Debussy's 'Clair de Lune,' " and that I came in third. He could be right; over the years I seem to have moved it up a notch.

The Apollo has been through difficult times. In the early 1950s, the management presented thirty shows a week, including Amateur Night on Wednesday and a midnight performance on Saturday. But in the sixties the enormous appeal of rock concerts drew audiences away to larger halls. In 1966, when the Harlem riots erupted, with fires and destruction, angry crowds respected the Apollo and left it untouched, but in January of 1976, because of financial difficulties, the Apollo, and, with it, Amateur Night, closed. A month earlier, during a Smokey Robinson concert, a shoot-out had occurred in which a man was killed and two people were wounded, and public confidence in the family atmosphere of the Apollo diminished. It reopened soon afterward as a theater showing mostly monster and B movies. Only occasionally were concerts booked. In 1981, the, theater went into bankruptcy. Eventually, the Inner City Broadcasting Corporation, led by the former Manhattan borough president Percy Sutton, bought the Apollo and spent twenty million dollars on restoring it as an entertainment complex, including sound studios and video-production facilities. They were seldom used. In June of 1983, the Apollo was granted landmark status, and on Christmas Eve of that year Amateur Night was started up again in the main theater. Wednesday night was invariably sold out, but in 1992, because of financial strain, the investors transferred ownership to a nonprofit organization, the Apollo Theater Foundation. The Sutton interests retained a television program they had started, *Showtime at the Apollo*, which still appears these days in eighty or so markets around the country (following *Saturday Night Live* in New York). In it Sandman Sims is on hand as the Executioner, rushing out during the Amateur Night part of the show.

Prompted by the mention of Amateur Night in the Ella Fitzgerald obituaries, I visited the Apollo late one Wednesday afternoon a few weeks after her death. I had forgotten what an admirable theater it is—surely one of New York City's great public places, with its long red-carpeted vestibule below a string of chandeliers, its Wall of Fame display of black stars who have performed on its stage, and then the theater itself, with its graceful lines and its ornate proscenium.

I was taken in hand by Grace Blake, the executive director of the Apollo Theater Foundation, who had been on the job for about nine months, after almost twenty-five years in the film industry. She explained that the goals of the foundation—besides continuing the Amateur Night tradition—were to revitalize the Apollo as a first-rate performing-arts center and to promote the musical heritage of African-Americans through live performances, recordings, television, and film. "The facilities here—the soundstage and the recording studios built by the Sutton group—are a perfect setup for such a program. It's a shame that up until now the complex has hardly ever been used," she said. I asked if whites had begun to come back to the Amateur Night performances. "Not New Yorkers," she said. "We get many Japanese and a few Germans. What a shame." She leaned back in her chair and exclaimed, "Oh, I'd like to invite the whole white world to come to the Apollo!" Born in Venezuela and brought up in Trinidad, Blake has a Caribbean lilt to her voice, which made the appeal all the more inviting.

I asked if the Japanese ever performed.

"Oh, yes," she said. She mentioned the Harmonica Boy, a young Japanese kid, not much older than six, who had played the blues. "The Japanese love plain old theatrical black music—blues, jazz," she explained. "One night, a Japanese singer sang 'Purple Rain,' by Prince. He couldn't speak English, but he'd learned all the words. Very strange accent. At the end, trying to sound like a rap artist, the young man riffed a bunch of four-letter swearwords, though it was clear he had no idea what he was saying."

I stayed around that evening. At about seven o'clock, the lobby began to fill: there were a lot of bare midriffs, and large gold earrings seemed to be the jewelry of choice. Japanese families lined up to have their pictures taken in front of the Wall of Fame.

Ms. Blake introduced me to a Japanese man named Tommy Tomita. He turned out to be largely responsible for the disproportionate number of his countrymen who come to the Apollo every Wednesday night. He told me that he had arrived in the United States about ten years before, with his wife, Miki Sakaguchi, who possessed a lovely singing voice. Enchanted by the gospel choirs she heard in Harlem, she had rather nervously put together a repertoire to compete on Amateur Night. She has won nine prizes, Tomita told me. He eventually wrote a guidebook about Harlem, and it became a great success in Tokyo—selling more than two hundred thousand copies a year—and that is why the Apollo ranks right up there with the Empire State Building and the Statue of Liberty on Japanese itineraries. The Japanese theatergoers arrive in yellow buses and sit together in a large block of seats on the right-hand side of the orchestra. If they approve of the performer, they shout "Hai! Hai!" Disapproval brings out a chorus of what sounded to my uneducated ear like "Boorrr! Boorr!"

I stood at the back of the house with Ms. Blake. The master of ceremonies checked out where the audience was from. "Let's hear it from the brothers and sisters from Manhattan," he began, and he moved on to the Bronx, Queens, Brooklyn, and finally to Staten Island, Long Island, and—to get a laugh—Rikers Island. He asked, "Minnesota?" One clap. And then "Japan?" A roar: "Hai! Hai!"

After everything had quieted down, we had a moment of silence in memory of Ella Fitzgerald, and it was followed by a rendition of her first hit, "A-Tisket, A-Tasket," by the four members of the house band, Ray Chew and the Crew.

The quality of the amateur performers was higher than I had expected. Indeed, Crowd Pleaser Lacey came out only once—to remove a rapper who was dressed in a cardiganlike sweater reaching below his knees and a cap turned backward. At the whine of the siren, Lacey appeared on a crutch, wearing his multicolored wig and three ties.

Next, a young woman, obviously nervous, struggled her way through "Amazing Grace."

I said to Ms. Blake that I was surprised the Executioner hadn't come for her.

"Well, you can't boo God or Jesus," she explained. "So the gospel singers most likely survive." A song that rarely gets hooted down, she said, however badly it is rendered, is "Jesus on the Main Line"—about His phone line, which is never busy—and she recalled one Amateur Gospel Night, when a rapper came onstage, rapped about God, and won first prize. "I was shocked," she said.

At the end of each act, the amateur made a rather clumsy bow—a head bob and a slight hitch of the body. Bowing was not something the contestants had worked on. I remembered my own awkward attempt.

At one point, a young man dressed in white flannels and a V-neck sweater touched the Tree of Hope and, after being introduced, launched into the Stevie Wonder song "Lately." I thought his Bill Tilden–like outfit would doom him, but his voice, strong and confident, not only won over the audience but brought Eva, Miss Apollo, out of her seat, up over the footlights, and onto the stage. He struggled both with her and with the end of "Lately," and managed to get out a tremulous final note as, in a delirium of affection, she flung an arm around his throat.

I was enjoying myself. I had noticed immediately how friendly the place had become. Two or three strangers came up to ask if I was having a good time. I said, "Oh, yes." I pointed to the stage and said I had been up there once.

"You're foolin'."

"I won second or third prize," I said. "I can't really remember which."

The New Yorker,
JANUARY 20, 1997

I, Bon Vivant

The other day a friend of mine telephoned—my literary agent actually—and remarked cheerily, "Well, how's the bon vivant today?"

At the time I had just come off the last week of jury duty and had ridden uptown in a dense and damp crowd on the Lexington Avenue subway. Out on the street it was raining slightly. The pavement was wet. Because of small holes in the soles of both shoes I walked along on my heels to avoid the water getting through and permeating my socks. The rain increased, and I took refuge in a Häagen-Dazs ice-cream parlor long enough to feel I should purchase something. I bought a chocolate ice-cream bar. Outside, I bit down on the bar, which had been frozen so hard that I broke off a tooth—one of the incisors. Unbelieving, I felt the gap in the front of my mouth, first with my tongue and then with my finger. No doubt at all. I had lost a tooth to the Häagen-Dazs ice-cream bar!

In a rage I took the offending bar by its stick, and, like skipping a stone, I scaled it down the length of the sidewalk. It behaved beautifully. Just off the pavement it went sailing by a man walking a dog.

"I lost a tooth," I said to my agent.

"Defending your honor, no doubt."

I've forgotten what else we talked about that day. But later on, sitting in the dentist's chair having the tooth replaced, I began pondering being referred to as a "bon vivant." Did I fit? I got to thinking about those I would consider bons vivants (besides myself, of course), some of whom I've known over the years. The name Serge Obolensky kept coming to mind. Needle-thin, always impeccably dressed, possessed of a trimmed mustache and a rather high, nasal, aristocratic voice, he seemed to me the embodiment of elegance and grace. A great partygoer and -giver, he was in the business of tonying up some of the great hotels of New York—among them the St. Regis, the Plaza, and the Sherry-Netherland.

A Russian-born prince (he claimed to be a descendant of Rurik, an early ruler of Russia), he preferred to be called Colonel. He was a cousin of Prince Felix Youssoupoff, in whose Saint Petersburg palace Rasputin was assassinated. In fact, Colonel Obolensky was there at the time. He described his involvement to me as we were driving down Park Avenue in a taxicab. I was particularly intrigued by the colonel's description of the conspirators pretending to hold a dance upstairs while, in a room below, Rasputin was being plied with Madeira laced with poison. The conspirators (the colonel among them) pounded their boots on the floor in time to the music from the windup phonograph machine, playing the same record over and over again.

"The poison didn't work, and we shot him as he came up the stairs," the colonel said. He was hard of hearing and he announced this in full cry. The cab gave a lurch, and I realized the driver had been listening. It is not often that one has a self-proclaimed murderer riding in the backseat.

The dentist took a wad of cotton out of my mouth. I said, "Not much glamour in losing a tooth to an ice-cream bar, is there? Should have had it knocked out in a barroom brawl. Hey, guess what? I knew the man who killed Rasputin."

"Open," the dentist said.

The novocaine began to take effect. I closed my eyes. Who else might fit the part of bon vivant? Cole Porter, certainly. He had lived the good life until that riding accident on the grounds of the Piping Rock Club on Long Island largely muzzled it. Born of wealth, which always helps, he had lived a most cultivated and adventurous life, at one point joining the French Foreign Legion. Afterward, he epitomized the Roaring Twenties (surely an era of *bon vivantisme*), as the titles of his hit shows suggest—*Anything Goes, Gay Divorce, Du Barry Was a Lady, Silk Stockings.* When I was a boy, I was trying to learn his haunting "Love for Sale" by heart on the piano. I was far too young to know what the song was about. My grandfather, a somewhat austere and difficult gentleman, overheard my attempts from the library and rang for the parlor maid.

She was instructed to go to the music room and tell me to cease and desist. No more "Love for Sale." My grandfather never came to tell me himself. Perhaps he thought he might have to explain *why* the song was unsuitable for a young boy.

I rinsed out into a porcelain sink. "Cole Porter," I announced. "Right at the top."

I sat back again and began thinking of Venice. When Cole Porter and his wife, Linda Lee Thomas, stayed at Venice's Rezzonico Palace, they entertained lavishly there, thinking nothing of inviting the Monte Carlo ballet for their guests' enjoyment. An elderly friend of mine once described a treasure hunt the Porters had arranged throughout Venice, the guests searching out the clues by gondola. I can't recall the particulars of the hunt, but I do remember her telling me that her gondolier had become quite caught up in the spirit of the chase and in rounding a corner had lost control of his oar in the darkness and tumbled into the canal.

Who else? A somewhat more sinister vision of the bon vivant came to mind. A few days before I went on jury duty I met a gentleman in his thirties, quite worldly, sleek-haired, sharp-featured, designer jeans, a soft white shirt. I was seated next to him on a banquette in a fancy late-hours bar in New York called Morgans—a place lit entirely by votive candles. In their light his shirt seemed to glow. He reminded me of a boulevardier dressed for a duel.

Oliver Stone, the filmmaker, was in our party. So were two or three young models, one of them a beautiful Russian girl. Her jeans were worn through at the knees so her pale skin showed, which was the fashion, of course. She spoke very little English.

At one point I asked the gentleman seated next to me if he minded my asking what he did. His reply was delivered slightly contemptuously, as if he *did* mind being asked. He said, "Well, I like the resort places when they are in season. Biarritz, Cannes, Monte Carlo, Aspen. I like small amounts of very good food." He had a faint Continental accent. "I like nightclubs, the best of them, like this, candles, dark. I like to seduce very young girls." He said this last without a trace of humor, as if speaking about something quite sacred to him. I was tempted to ask him if the beautiful young Russian girl was young enough for his designs. Instead, I said, "My, quite the bon vivant."

"I would think so," he said.

It occurred to me that this fellow would have fit quite nicely into the Regency period. Perhaps he would end up like the duke of Queensberry, known as Old Q, a great rake of the time—a familiar sight in his seventies, sitting on his London balcony; below, a servant was kept on alert to hop on a horse and take after anyone Old Q especially fancied.

"Rinse, please."

I thought of Beau Brummell, of course, the leader of the London beaux . . . that fraternity of reckless, gay, adventurous, dissipated, witty men around town. Lord Byron was a great admirer of

Brummell's. Indeed he once said that the three great men of his time were Brummell, Napoleon, and himself. Brummell, of course, was especially noted as a fashion plate; it was said that he had two makers for his gloves—one for the thumbs, the other for the rest of the hand. He spent two hours daily—after cleaning his teeth and shaving—in scrubbing himself with a pig's-bristle brush and working over his eyebrows and whiskers with a dentist's mirror and tweezers before he ever considered getting into his clothes.

Neckwear had to be starched, tied, and creased perfectly or it was discarded. A story went the rounds that Brummell's valet, coming down the staircase from his master's dressing room, remarked on the armful of ties he was carrying as "our failures." Three barbers were on hand to do Brummell's hair, and his boots—including their soles—were polished with the froth of champagne. On his daily walk he never took off his hat because replacing it exactly as it had been, just so, was unlikely. He was so fastidious at his dress, and knew so much about fashion, that the Prince of Wales was once reduced to "blubbering" when told that Brummell did not like the cut of his coat.

Much of this is probably exaggeration. One felicitous observation about Brummell was that he escaped notice because he fitted the landscape with delicate exactitude. Somebody once remarked to him that an acquaintance was so well dressed that people turned around to gaze after him. "Then," said Brummell, "he is *not* well dressed."

A minor thing I remembered about Brummell was that among the items on his dressing table was a spitting dish made of silver, as porcelain was too déclassé. It crossed my mind to tell the dentist this, but I resisted.

"Open wide. Turn this way a bit."

My favorite peer of that time, and certainly a candidate in the bon vivant business, was Henry de la Pier Beresford, the marquis of Waterford, often known as the Mad Marquis. He was not only interested in the usual pleasures of life but for reasons best known to himself he had a strong desire to see two locomotives smash into each other. He wrote the following letter to the officials of the London and Greenwich Railway Company:

> Sirs:
> I am anxious to witness a train smash. If you will allow two of your engines to collidc, head on, at full speed, I will contribute a sum of 10,000 £s to your funds.
> Waterford

The London and Greenwich officials wrote back and refused, implying in their letter that Waterford belonged in an institution. The peer was not deterred in the slightest. He managed to buy a pair of decrepit engines, and on a friend's estate, which included a spur of track, he built a small pavilion for friends and for the bestowing of champagne and so forth. The day of the smash was fine, the marquis's elegant guests in good form; but, alas, at the appointed moment the empty engines drew toward the pavilion at different speeds. One of them, its throttle fixed too far forward, sped by; there was a fine bonging sound back behind a hill, and all Waterford and his friends got to see was a distant plume of steam.

The dentist's assistant appeared. She was perhaps a bit old for my boulevardier friend of the nightclubs, but very pretty nonetheless, and I felt vaguely embarrassed as she bent close and peered into my open mouth.

"Aaargh," I said.

As I looked up at her, it occurred to me that one does not often speak of the *bonne vivante*, the female representative of the species. A few names came to mind as I sat back. Surely toward the top of the list would be the late Marjorie Merriweather Post, heiress to the Post cereal fortune and noted especially for her years as a hostess. In Washington, invitations to her parties were second only to those from the White House. One synopsis of her life described her as a "financier, philanthropist, horticulturalist, hostess, square-dance enthusiast, and former amateur boxer." She got an enormous pleasure out of life. People said of her that when she walked into a room, everyone else looked exhausted. Years ago I went to one of her dances at Mar-A-Lago in Palm Beach. Sure enough, there was an instructor to tell us how to lineup for the Virginia reels and so on. I barely remember Mrs. Post. It seems to me she was sitting in a large chair and didn't join in. If I'd known then about her boxing past, I would have gone over and asked about it.

I would suppose Perle Mesta is a good candidate. When she was very young, growing up in Oklahoma City, she was given a birthday party to which no one came. She often said that back then she had vowed, weeping, that she would eventually give parties to which "the mostes' " people in the world would come. And indeed they did—sometimes as many as eight hundred to her Washington estate, Les Ormes. She had her detractors: A rival hostess referred to her as "The Thing." But a friend, the writer Louis Bromfield, described her as "one of the gayest people I know—she could give you a good time if she had only a five-cent beer."

Mesta's counterpart in New York was Kitty Miller, the wife of Gilbert Miller, the theater producer. She gave sought-after New Year's Eve parties. I remember going to one in the fifties. I had a little tin trumpet. At the stroke of midnight I noticed that Salvador Dalí was standing next to me in the crowd. He was famously distinguished by a waxed mustache that curled up at both ends. Undoubtedly invigorated by the Millers' end-of-the-year champagne, I bent down on impulse and, placing the bell of the little trumpet over one tip of his mustache, I blew a blast. What I remember about that moment is that Dalí didn't flinch. When I pulled away, it was evident that the mustache had not been affected in the slightest.

The dentist snapped off his gloves. "I wouldn't recommend eating for a few hours," he said.

Most people equate the bon vivant with eating—with gourmandising, the love of good fare. To pick a name at random I would suppose Edward VII makes the roster. After all, on one of his visits to Monte Carlo he supposedly presided over the invention of a dish whose name combined quite nicely his love of both food and women: crêpes Suzette—Suzette being one of his favorite mistresses.

So how does one arrive at a notion of the bon vivant from the above? The idea suggests wealth, a bit of time on one's hands, an ability to get along on three hours' sleep at night (or during the day, so that the night is free for carousing), a zest for good food, a knowledge of fine wines, and, most important of all, a supercilious manner that suggests there is absolutely nothing special about this style of life at all. It can be dangerous: Witness one of the eulogies at Truman Capote's funeral (surely a practitioner himself of the good life), namely the statement that Capote had died from living.

It helps, of course, to be endowed with above-average energy and vim, what the French refer to as élan. My favorite exemplar of this was Augustus the Strong of Saxony, a suitably named German prince of the early eighteenth century, said to have been famous for two parlor tricks. The first was to ride a horse bareback into a barn and chin himself on a crossbeam, gripping the horse between his knees. The second was to appear before the lady of his choice, holding a bag of gold in one hand and crushing a horseshoe with the other. He reputedly had 367 illegitimate children (among them a future *maréchal* of France), which would suggest that the latter stratagem was extremely successful.

Now, what do I have in common with these worthies? I have no intention of dashing into a barn and chinning myself on a crossbeam, with or without a horse between my knees. I have very little interest in clothes and have been known to wear a seersucker suit in the dead of winter. I have never murdered a monk.

Perhaps *bon vivantisme* is only in the eye of the beholder. So the other day I called my agent.

"Hey," I said. "It's the bon vivant."

"Of course," he said. "Who else?"

Gourmet,
FEBRUARY 1998

A Day in the Life . . .

—

I get up around eight and eat a breakfast of bran flakes, an English muffin with marmalade, and a coffee substitute named Pero which I've come to like the taste of. I read the *New York Times*, mulling over the sports section and the letters opposite the Op Ed page—the latter tend to provide an interesting subtext to what's in the rest of the paper.

Then I sit down at my desk and try to work. I am finishing a book about Truman Capote—an oral biography. It's not really writing as much as stitching—trying to meld together into a unified flow segments from hundreds of interviews. I use a lot of Scotch tape and a scissors is always at hand. If laid out, a finished chapter, unrolled, could stretch the length of a couple of rooms. It's the third oral biography I've worked on—the other two (with Jean Stein) being *Edie*, which is about Edie Sedgwick, the Andy Warhol superstar, and *American Journey: The Times of Robert F. Kennedy*, about the senator, a classmate of mine at Harvard. Another book which I've edited, also based on interviews but presented in the more usual form, is *D.V.*, Diana Vreeland's autobiography. Both *D.V.* and *Edie* were on the bestseller list, and of course I hope the same for the work on Truman, as yet untitled. I knew him fairly well. I was invited to his Black and White Ball. He lived down the road when I had a house in Sagaponack. But then I did something that put quite a strain on our friendship. I wrote a parody based on the conceit that Truman couldn't finish his novel *Answered Prayers* and had reverted to another writer's style in the hopes of doing so. Stutterers do this; they pick another accent and it works for a while. The writer Truman Capote had picked was Ernest Hemingway, so what you had was the odd combination of Hemingway's style and Truman's sensibilities. My parody was called *The Snows of Studiofiftyfour.* You'll remember that in Hemingway's *The Snows of Kilimanjaro* the protagonist is lying on a cot, his leg gangrenous, waiting to be flown back to Nairobi. In the story he thinks back on his life and his contemporaries. In my version Truman is in the San Diego airport waiting to be flown back to New York. He has just been to a fat farm where he had his face and his behind lifted. He too thinks back on his enemies. I thought at the time it was one of the best things I've ever done. It was published in *Harper's Magazine.* Truman thought otherwise (who can blame him!) and it was uncomfortable being in the same room with him, the target of that voice of his. They used to say that his voice was so high that only dogs could hear it, but I can vouch that's not so!

So in the morning I fuss away with *Truman*, cutting and pasting. There are any number of diversions. Two very young twin daughters, Laura and Olivia. They are lurching toward two years old. Both are fascinated by books. So I read to them—books that are six pages long with pages made of wood. When they are taken by their mother to the beach, and it's quiet, I often break away from *Truman* to thump on the piano, a Baldwin. I fancy original compositions full of arpeggios and chords in the minor key. An opera singer lives down the bay a bit, and I suspect she closes the window when the sounds drift her way. Sometimes I can't resist it and I join the rest of the family at the beach on Gardiners Bay for a swim. I don't swim out too far, preferring to reach down and touch the bottom. If it's sunny we'll sit there, swatting the occasional horsefly, and watch the children rush around.

Around midmorning I go back and I feed the seagull. He comes and perches on a piling. I go out on the afterdeck (we live on a landlocked barge with the stern over the water) and I pitch him a piece of bread. We've given him a name but I've forgotten which one it is—either Roscoe, Oscar, or Olly.

Sometimes, over a spit of land that encloses Accabonac Bay I can see the terns working the water outside, which means that bluefish most likely are driving bait fish up to the surface. So I hop down into my little fifteen-foot Boston Whaler and go out to baitcast for them. On the way out I pass a little cluster of lobster boats with names like *Mary E.*, *Jane W.*, *Ellen S.* on their sterns, but one of them boldly carries the name *WHORE*, and that's something to brood about while fishing—how things are getting along in *that* family!

For lunch I usually have a bacon, lettuce, and tomato sandwich with mayonnaise on white toast. I get in my old Army jeep (vintage 1972) and drive down to the Springs General store to pick it up. Sometimes I go to eat the sandwich in the Green River Cemetery—a tiny parcel of land which includes many of the Abstract Expressionist school—Pollock, Krasner, et al.—and so exclusive that it is jokingly said that people die to get in there. Visitors place little icons on the gravestones, mostly pebbles, but I have seen paintbrushes, used paint tubes, parts of palettes, as if these homages might procure a bit of luck from the interred. I sit in the grass and worry about finishing *Truman.*

In the afternoon I try to pick up a tennis game, preferably with my son Taylor who is nineteen, a fine player, quick as a minnow, and who now slaughters me. I don't mind, though perhaps he does, because he has a good soul, and he calls across, "great shot!" when I have made a mediocre one.

Back at the barge it's time to rest up a bit after all that exercise. I read. I read the magazines I write for—*Sports Illustrated, Harper's, The New Yorker*, and a lot of those I don't: *Time, Newsweek*, the *Atlantic Monthly*, the *Nation*, the *New Republic.* I read manuscripts for the magazine I work for—*The Paris Review.* The barge has a superb library. I take down a book and there goes another hour or so. I reread Barbara Tuchman's *The Guns of August* last month . . . marveling not only at the style but at the enormity of research and wondering if I have done enough for the Truman Capote book.

Then comes the evening. Accabonac Bay is famous for its sunsets. The Abstract Expressionists and their friends brought their evening picnics and drinks down to the Bay to watch them. We do the same. With our feet up on the railing at the stern of the barge, we watch the sun drop below Wood Tick Island. The twins arrive with their six-page books. The Black Skimmers sail by—extraordinary birds that fish by trailing their lower bills in the water, leaving a slight wake like a thin pencil stroke on the surface.

There are the evening parties of course. Last week we went to a party at Jimmy Buffett's house in North Haven. Big fan-backed armchairs set about the lawn in the deep twilight. Interesting friends—the Isham brothers, P. J. O'Rourke, Peter Maas, Steve Croft, Richard Price, Conrad Cafritz, all with their wives. Lobsters, clams, and corncobs for dinner. Many of the writers chat about projects that are due. I hum nervously and think back on how I've wasted the day, the folders with Truman Capote material within hardly touched. I have a drink. It's Capote's kind of party. The house is a wonder in itself. White-painted, with porches fronting both floors, it looks as if it had been plucked out of a posh section of Charleston, South Carolina, and set down on wide lawns that slope gradually to the waters of the Sound: Jay Gatsby's name must have been whispered a hundred times that night.

It's a bit intimidating to leave such a place to return to the somewhat confined space of our barge. But we have a last drink on the afterdeck with our feet up. It's almost the time in August for the Pleiades meteor showers. The activity up there is increasing, and we wait until we have seen three of them streaking across the sky before going to bed.

New York Post,
AUGUST 18, 1996

Waiting for Gannon

—

In March I got a call from the *Late Night with David Letterman* show from a Mr. Frank Gannon, a producer and what is known in the talk-show trade as a segment coordinator. I was out of town at the time, but the message was that he had an interest in the column I had written in these pages about April Fools' Day, and he left a number to call. From this I deduced they wanted me as a guest on their April 1 show to chat about famous practical jokes and hoaxes and so on with Mr. Letterman—appropriate enough, since he strikes me as the type who wishes every day could be lived as April Fools' Day.

When I telephoned and said I was returning the producer's call, I was told that Mr. Gannon was "on the floor" somewhere but couldn't be found. Well, that's too bad, I said, and left the message that I was back in town and expected to hear from him.

Nothing happened for a few days. Impelled by curiosity, I began to put in calls to him. Sometimes I was told he was in a meeting. More often, he was "somewhere about" and couldn't be found. After a while Mr. Gannon began to emerge in my mind's eye as a shadowy, furtive man with so much on his mind about co-ordinating segments that he was last seen scuttling up and down the back fire stairs, slipping in and out of large packing boxes. A kind of phantom figure haunting the mausolean gloom of the NBC soundstages, he left just an occasional trace to indiciate that in fact he did exist—a half-eaten sandwich, a single shoe out of which he had stepped in his haste to avoid contact with the outside world.

I realized, of course, after perhaps the twenty-first call, that I was getting what's called the old runaround—my presence was not wanted on Mr. Letterman's show on April 1 or any other time. Mr. Gannon was telling me this by refusing to do so—a spineless procedure that is typical in show business. His tribe seems incapable of saying into a phone: "Hey, thanks for calling but we can't use you," or whatever. Instead, they hide in their packing cases.

I suspect a scholarly treatise could be written about show business and the phone. The telephone is theoretically a means of communication. Not so in television or movieland. Nobody I know is listed, whatever their professional standing—assistant director, cameraman, gaffer, best boy, et al.—as being unlisted is apparently a sign of status. If your name is in the Beverly Hills/Hollywood directory it means you're unimportant and probably out of work.

There are so few pages that it is by far the easiest telephone directory, if one is up to such strong-man tricks, to tear in half. The result of all this is that nobody can reach anybody, which is why things are as bad as they are out there.

It's very hard for me to understand this. Nobody dares come to the phone! Think of the missed opportunities! Suppose in Mr. Gannon's case I was trying to get a message to him that Kim Basinger had spotted him in the shadows of a packing case during a *Late Night* appearance and had been absolutely smitten but was too timid to call him on her own.

Ah, well. I kept calling Mr. Gannon right up to April 1. I had an entire lineup of entertaining pranks to describe to Letterman. A friend in London was poised to send me the latest of the hoaxes that invariably appear in the newspapers there on April Fools' Day so that I could describe them that evening. (A few years ago he sent me from one of the dailies an article titled "The Dark Side of the World of Beatrix Potter" that described horrendous goings-on in the private life of the gentle inventor of Peter Rabbit.)

So I had all this to offer . . . and if Letterman was pleased and things were rolling along, I could tell him about an extraordinary hoax recounted to me by Michael Arlen, the *New Yorker* writer and an old friend. It involved his father, a very celebrated fellow in his time. Mr. Arlen was the author of an enormously successful novel titled *The Green Hat.* He was very much the expatriate dandy; indeed, he introduced Duff Twysden to Ernest Hemingway, who later immortalized her as Lady Brett in *The Sun Also Rises.* Michael wrote a lovely memoir about his father, titled *Exiles*. Here is the gist of what he wrote me about the hoax:

"Did I ever tell you about the time I was forced to hire false parents? In the early Fifties I was in the Army in Europe, first with *Stars & Stripes* in Germany and then in London, where my boss was a certain Brigadier General O. K. Wilmerding. Actually I was not supposed to be in London and this is where my problems began. I was supposed to be stationed outside London at an Air Force base from which I could most easily cover the Air Force golf tournaments for *Stars & Stripes.* Golf, you see, occupied such a large part of General Wilmerding's thoughts.

"As it happened, I was actually living in a little third-floor walk-up in Brompton Square, because the week I arrived in England my father, also in London, had become sick, and I was given permission by General Wilmerding's deputy to attend him, so to speak. Thus my flat in Brompton Square and my daily commute back and forth to the air base, a very agreeable arrangement for all concerned.

"Then, alas, all too rapidly, my father recovered and returned to New York. Had I been made of better stuff I would have told General Wilmerding. But I didn't. He had other things to worry about—war, golf, and so on. But I hadn't reckoned on his secret yearning for the cosmopolitan life, for what used to be called rubbing shoulders with celebrities. At first it was casual asides: 'How's the old man?' Then: 'I bet your old man knows a lot of famous people.' Then: 'Say, Arlen, I'd really like to meet your old man—of course, when he's feeling better.' Of course. Maybe I could persuade my father to come back to London and meet General Wilmerding. Not bloody likely. Besides, my father hated generals, so the meeting, if it had occurred, would not have been a success. Maybe I could tell General Wilmerding that my father had died. Suddenly. Tragically. But Wilmerding would want to go to the funeral in the event it might be attended by famous people.

"For a long time I did nothing, hoping the problem would go away. But it didn't. One day Wilmerding came up to me with ominous good cheer. 'I'm going into London this afternoon. I thought I'd give your father a call.' I thought of saying, 'Oh, no, he's just taken a turn for the worse. The doctor says no phone calls.' But this was just stalling. So I devised the party.

"Ken Tynan, the theater critic, helped me find the actors—a wonderful fellow named Charlie Banksmith to play my father, a woman called Edie somebody to play my mother. I remember thinking how completely horrified my parents would have been—but what did it matter, I reasoned. General Wilmerding had never seen them, never seen photographs. He only wanted to rub shoulders.

"I hired two rooms at the Dorchester for an afternoon and an additional half dozen actors who looked like important people. I asked such friends as I could muster and invited General and Mrs. O. K. Wilmerding. Was it a success? Well, I think it was. There was a dangerous moment when my 'father,' clearly drunk, started making passes at Mrs. Wilmerding. I had to take him aside and tell him to get back in character. But Wilmerding himself didn't seem to mind. I think he probably felt that having his wife pinched was a treat for both of them—a rare glimpse of life at the top, the decadence of famous people and so on. The whole thing seems to me quite amazing as I think about it now. Rented parents!

"At any rate, I got to keep my little flat in Brompton Square, from which I sashayed out early in the morning to cover the many golfing missions. When my father did die two years later I remember my mother showing me what she described as the 'sweetest, strangest letter' she had received from some people called Wilmerding in Texas. ' "What good times we all had together in London," ' she said, quoting from the letter. 'What do you suppose they meant by that?' "

Armed with this material, I telephoned *Late Night* as often as three times a day as April 1 approached. I continued to say that I was returning Mr. Gannon's call, which I thought created a proper sense of urgency. Always at the other end they were very polite, and then came the long wait while they went off looking for him. I imagined them catching a glimpse of a vanishing back and calling after him: "Gannon! Gannon!" Always they came back on the line and said he was out on the floor somewhere. . . .

Once I called and said: "This is Gannon. I'm out on the floor somewhere. Can you tell me where?"

I could hear someone breathing at the other end of the line.

"*Late Night*," a voice said tentatively.

I even tried on the morning of April 1. My London friend had called to give me the hoaxes from the morning dailies. The best was from the *Daily Mail*, reporting that Stonehenge was about to be dismantled and moved to a new site. The original plan was to move everything to Snowdon, but a Japanese consortium had entered the picture—offering 480 billion yen to move Stonehenge to Mount Fuji!

I thought Mr. Gannon would be amused. But no luck. This time I was told he was in a meeting. It crossed my mind that his staff had finally collared him in the back of a packing case and was wrestling him into a backstage closet.

I watched the show that night from a hotel room in Chicago. I left a party early to see what Mr. Gannon had preferred to my April Fools' stuff. I turned on the set. Well, no wonder! April 1, a Monday, turned out to be a rerun night! Out-of-date jokes about Cher, Dan Quayle. A very funny comic, Martin Short, came on and there was banter about Letterman's tie (a yellowish hue) and the fact that Short wasn't wearing one. The exchanges were quick and lively, like tennis pros volleying with each other at net. Not my sort of pace at all. I tend to cross my legs, lean back, and dawdle. Letterman would have fidgeted during my splendid Arlen material.

Still, why hadn't Mr. Gannon come to the phone to tell me that he'd discovered there wasn't an April Fools' show? So simple. It confirmed my suspicion that he's in trouble out there on the floor somewhere. I've called a few times since. Being a fireworks buff I have some ideas to offer the show on July Fourth. No luck. Can't find him. He's vanished. If you're as worried as I am about Mr. Gannon, call NBC—in New York the number is listed. Or perhaps call the police.

Esquire,
JULY 1991

My Last Cobra

—

The trouble began on a bird-watching expedition to India and the mountain kingdom of Bhutan a year and a half ago when I developed an aggravated bursitis condition in my left elbow. Fortunately, a doctor was on the expedition, and one evening he lanced my elbow, which looked as though a Ping-Pong ball had been inserted in it. But the relief was only temporary. When we came out of the Black Mountains of Bhutan, my arm had swollen to such proportions that I was forced to loosen my watch strap a couple of holes. At the Adventist Hospital in Bangkok, the elbow, now almost the size of a tennis ball, was lanced again by my doctor friend.

Back in New York the elbow was lanced yet again and my arm set in a cast and a sling. Around town, when asked what was wrong, I replied, "Oh, it's an aggravated bursitis condition. Nothing serious."

Then I made a mistake. It occurred at a cocktail party given by Alexander Chancellor, then the editor of the "Talk of the Town" department of *The New Yorker.* The usual inquiries were being made about my arm. I thanked those who asked and said it was nothing to worry about—a simple aggravated bursitis condition. Sometimes, if they stayed around, I talked about the cranes we'd seen in India—the rare Siberian, and the Sarus cranes that stand as tall as a man. If the guests stared at my arm in its sling, I talked about the low medical costs in Thailand. (The cost of the facilities given my doctor for the procedure, including nurses, syringes, antibiotics, a sling, and a safety pin to hold it: $40.)

About midway through the party I caught sight of Jason Epstein standing by the door putting on his coat to leave. He is a senior editor at Random House. He called out, "Hey, George, what's wrong with your arm?"

Suddenly, it seemed too boring to give the usual answer. So somewhat to my own astonishment I found myself saying over the chatter of the party: "Well, Jason, the damnedest thing. I was lying in some tall grass at the Bharatpur Reserve, peering at a pair of Sarus cranes through my binoculars, when I sensed some movement to my left. I turned, raised my arm, and was bitten in the elbow by a small cobra!"

Jason's eyes widened. "My God!" he exclaimed. His date, standing beside him, said, "Hey, Jason, we're late!" and before I could admit I was joshing him she had propelled him out the door.

My immediate reaction was one of dismay. Jason is a familiar and popular figure at various social and publishing functions and watering holes around the city. It was inevitable that the cobra story would quickly get about.

Two days later the phone rang, and a man I didn't know came on. "Hey," he said. "I was having lunch with Elizabeth Sifton, the editor at Farrar, Straus and Giroux, today, and she tells me that you've been bitten by a cobra." By the most extraordinary coincidence, it turned out the caller was a doctor of considerable reputation, formerly the head of New York City's Roosevelt Hospital, and an expert on poisons and toxins, including snake venoms. He would be most pleased if I could have lunch with him to discuss what had happened.

This would have been the appropriate time for me to admit that I had been kidding about the cobra. Instead, my heart pounding and my face reddening, I told the doctor that it had been a *small* cobra, really nothing, that my recovery had been swift, without complications, not much to report . . .

"Oh no!" the doctor said, insisting that anything I could tell him about the incident would be of great value to him. "Please."

I couldn't get out of it. I said that if he really wished, I'd be delighted to have lunch with him in three or four weeks—setting a considerable period of time so that in the interim he might forget that we had a date. We chatted for a while about Gaboon vipers. He sounded as though he could hardly wait for our lunch.

—

His was the first of a number of calls, enough to make me realize the situation had truly gotten out of hand. I decided to explain matters to my mother, who is ninety-three. She is active in New York social circles—bridge clubs, charity luncheons—and soon enough she would hear that her son had been bitten by a cobra.

So we had lunch. She noticed my arm sling but didn't seem especially curious about it.

"Mother," I said. "You're going to hear about this arm of mine . . . that I've been bitten on the elbow by a small cobra." I waited a beat. I couldn't resist it. "Mother, it's true."

"Stuff and nonsense," she said. "You have an aggravated bursitis condition."

Astonished, I asked, "How do you know?"

"Why, I saw your doctor at a concert two evenings ago," she said. "You might have told me when you got back from India," she went on reproachfully. "It's awkward to hear about such things from others."

The next day my sister called. "Hey!" she said. "I hear you've been bitten by a cobra on the elbow."

"Who told you that?"

"Mother," she said.

It turns out that my mother rather liked the cobra-bite story. I could imagine her sitting down at the bridge table, shuffling the cards, and getting ready to tell her friends, which she does by clearing her throat to get attention.

The cobra story was not only hers to tell. It got into the newspapers. New York's *Daily News* had an item in its gossip column. One paper reported that I was recovering in a hospital in Nairobi, Kenya, from a dangerous cobra bite suffered while on safari in Africa.

What was curious was that as time went on, the cobra experience began to become not only clear in my mind but secure, as if it had actually happened. I could almost smell the marsh grass on which I was lying, the feel of the earth against my belly, the faint movement of something off to my left. "Oh yes," I would say when asked, invariably emphasizing that it had been a *small* cobra. To my shame, I felt no qualms about perpetuating the untruth. After all, I reasoned, it was verified in the nation's press—it had gone out over the wire. The item was now tucked away in countless newspaper files, perhaps to reemerge at my demise: MAN WHO SURVIVED COBRA BITE DIES.

The only individual I promised myself to come clean with was the doctor from Roosevelt Hospital. He had telephoned a few times since his last call and had not forgotten our luncheon date. Worried about his reaction, I had the inspired thought to have our lunch on April Fools' Day, hoping that he would accept what I had done in the spirit of that occasion. My plan was to lead him on throughout most of the meal . . . until the coffee, say, at which point I would lean forward and, in that sly, unctuous manner of the practical jokester about to break the news, ask the doctor if he realized what day it was.

To prepare for our meeting, I called up the Bronx Zoo to speak to someone in the herpetology department and find out what *does* happen to someone once bitten by a cobra.

The scientist was very forthcoming. "There's probably a burning sensation where the cobra bit," he said, "a tingling up the arms, on the lips, as well as evasive saliva. . . ."

"Evasive saliva?"

"Drooling, if you will. There have been reports of euphoria . . . hallucinations, and, of course, local neuropathy, especially around the lung area. That is how people die from a cobra bite—the neural system that works the lungs fails."

"The euphoria does not last for a long time."

"Absolutely not."

"Anything else?"

The scientist paused. "It appears that the vision is affected," he said. "Green leaves in a tree might appear to be red. Vision is likely to be blurred. Of course, all this depends on the severity of the bite. . . ."

The scientist didn't ask me why I wanted the information. I had planned to tell him I was working on a murder thriller in which a cobra is dropped through a trapdoor into a victim's bathtub. Lying was becoming appallingly easy to do.

The doctor and I had lunch at a midtown club. We sat at a window table for two. He was a large man, with a smile so friendly that I winced thinking what was going to happen to it once the news sank in.

Though the doctor had never traveled to Africa or Asia, continents with a plethora of cobras and other poisonous snakes, it turned out that he was the foremost authority in New York City on snakebites. "As a consultant to the City Department of Health, I'm okayed only for snakes," he told me. "It's not kosher for me to handle bites by lionfish, poison frogs, or any other deadly critters. Only snakes."

He had plenty to keep him busy. He said I would be surprised how many amateur collectors would take "difficult" snakes out of their herpetoriums to see how they'd get along on the living-room carpet. He described a baggage handler at JFK airport who, noticing a mild turmoil in a mail sack, had gone over to investigate and had been bitten by a king cobra through the canvas.

"Wow!"

"Astonishing to think you can order snakes through the mail," the doctor said. "You can find advertisements for this in magazines like *Field and Stream.* Here's an interesting case. A woman bought a leather coat that had been made in Okinawa. She developed a severe pain in the arm, and it turned out she had been bitten by a kind of Asian copperhead—a habu, it's called."

"A what?"

"A habu. It apparently was living in the lining of the coat."

"Wow!" I said for the second time. "How long do you think the habu was in there?"

"Quite a while, I would judge." The doctor smiled. "These

creatures are very self-sufficient. We had a case of someone who decided to help a cottonmouth shed its skin. They've been doing it successfully for three hundred million years. The kid thought the creature needed help and got bitten for his pains. Isn't that a beauty?"

By the time we'd finished the main course, the doctor had described a number of other instances, including an encounter between a biology teacher "who should have known better" and a saw-scaled viper, a Middle Eastern "creature."

"When this viper moves," the doctor explained, "its scales slide one over the other, which makes a quite distinctive sound . . . rather like the sound of Wheaties being crushed between the fingers, though, mind you, that's not a scientific description."

The doctor took a sip of water. He continued: "Anyway, that's why the biology teacher had this creature—an auditory pleasure for him—and when he poked it into motion so he could listen to it, it *got* him. Caused a severe blood disorder. Almost killed him."

"Wow!"

As the dessert arrived, the doctor leaned back in his chair, joined his fingers in a steeple, and asked me to tell him about my cobra. I cleared my throat. "Well, doctor, I was lying in some grass looking through my binoculars at a Sarus crane when I sensed some movement to my left and was bitten in the point of the elbow by this small cobra."

We discussed what kind of cobra it was.

"Small," I said. "Really quite small. You don't suppose it could have been a krait."

"Oh no," the doctor said. "Hardly possible. Almost undoubtedly, considering the area, a spectacled cobra."

I thought of the distinctive eye pattern on the back of that particular species' hood and shivered slightly as I reached for a corn muffin.

"And then?" The doctor's eyes glistened behind his glasses.

"I didn't run."

"Capital!" It turned out as our conversation progressed that "capital" (along with "creature" or "critter") was a favorite expression.

I continued: "My friend Peter Matthiessen was a half mile down the spillway, hoping to spot the Siberian crane out there in the marsh. Not much he could have done anyway."

"Of course not."

"So I sat down on a sort of knoll and took off the moleskin shirt I was wearing. I looked at my elbow and I could see that the bite was not so much a puncture as a small tear. There was discomfort, as if acid had been splashed on the wound, but this was counteracted"— I gulped slightly—"by an odd feeling of . . . what? . . . Exaltation? Euphoria? . . ."

"Capital!" the doctor exploded.

"Then I noticed something quite curious. The leaves—"

"Yes, the leaves," the doctor interjected.

"—the leaves on the trees overhead had turned reddish, a kind of autumnal color. Quite odd."

"Oh, this is truly splendid," said the doctor. The reason for his excitement—he went on to explain—was that a long-standing disagreement exists about the working of cobra poison on the human system. The question is whether it works its way up the brain stem and affects the brain itself. Many authorities believe it doesn't, that it simply does its damage below the neck. My description of the discolored leaves supported the doctor's hypothesis that the brain was involved.

"Go on," he said eagerly.

I couldn't bring myself to tell him that sitting there on the knoll I had begun to drool. Besides, the timing was perfect for me to lean forward and let him in on the gag. All I had to do was to remark somewhat roguishly, "Hey, doctor, do you know what day it is?"

I could not bring myself to do it. I have wondered since why I did not fess up. Perhaps it was because I feared that, at what Aristotle referred to as the "moment of recognition," the doctor would rear up out of his chair, aggrieved, with a terrible howl that would turn heads in the august and subdued atmosphere of that midtown men's club.

The other possibility was more upsetting: that I simply could not let it go. I truly liked the fact that my mother was spreading the story at her bridge meetings: "One spade. Have you heard what's happened to my son?"

I can't recall much more about the lunch other than the palpable delight the doctor showed on being told about the chameleonlike leaves.

—

Almost a year to the day after our April Fools' lunch at the club, I got a letter from the doctor. He said he was writing a long essay or perhaps a short book on his experiences with serious snakebite in an urban setting. Could he use my experience as an anecdote? Presumably he was going to enlist my evidence to support his views on the effect of cobra poison on the brain. I stared at the letter, appalled.

Eventually, a solution came to mind. I would write an account of everything that had happened: the bursitis condition in Bhutan, the arm in the sling, the cocktail party where I'd sprung the cobra-bite story on Jason Epstein, my mother's reaction, the call from the doctor—all this in careful detail, including a harsh look at my own lapses of judgment. When it was all typed up and given a title ("My Last Cobra") I'd send it off to the doctor, making sure that it got to him at some point on April 1. It occurred to me that it might be wise to send a bouquet of roses along as well.

All that was required was an envelope and some stamps. I had the good doctor's address. And yet there was this curious reluctance to let it go. What greater substantiation of what happened to me in the sedge grass at the Bharatpur Reserve than to have notice of it in an essay published, say, in a distinguished medical journal! I was tempted to send the doctor a wire: *By all means use what you wish stop delighted to contribute to medical knowledge stop please send copies of article when published*—this last so I could carry clippings from it around in my wallet to bring out at suitable occasions.

I did send the package, of course. In the days following I expected the doctor to write or call—either to express chagrin or, I hoped, to admit he'd been duped but no harm done. A month went by. Then another. An eerie silence. I don't dare call. I have been avoiding the club where we had lunch. If a package arrives in the mail, I shake it slightly to make sure that from within I don't hear a hiss, or a rattle, or, especially, the sound of Wheaties being crushed between the fingers. . . .

Harper's Magazine,
SEPTEMBER 1994

A Twisted Tale

—

At a black-tie fundraiser in Chicago for the Friends of Conservation not long ago, Jim Fowler, the famous wildlife educator and former host of *Wild Kingdom*, was on hand (wearing a safari jacket in lieu of a tuxedo) to show off a few of his charges. He brought out a capuchin monkey, a leopard, a Florida cougar, and a fifteen-foot Burmese python—a rare albino specimen, patterned a pale yellow and white.

After the applause had died away, back at his table Fowler was asked if he ever had trouble with large snakes. He smiled and said that he was reminded of an experience he'd had a few years ago with an anaconda from South America—about eighteen feet long—that he was planning to take to Johnny Carson's *Tonight Show.*

"It was the night before, and there I was in my room on the fourteenth floor of the Sheraton Universal in Burbank with my more than two-hundred-pound anaconda. He was covered with cedar chips from his ride in the suitcase, so I undressed and got into the bathtub with him to wash him down. After I swabbed him dry, I went to the door to get the newspaper that I had noticed on my way in. I had the anaconda on my shoulders at the time, and rather than put him back in the tub I carried him into the other room. The way you handle a big snake is to keep the top end around your shoulders; the rest of it will entwine around your stomach."

The guests nodded as if in concurence: "Of course, of course."

"I opened the door and reached down for the paper," Fowler continued. "On my neck, the anaconda shifted his weight forward, extending his neck out about six feet as a sort of counterbalance, which threw *me* off balance and I half-stumbled out into the corridor."

"Uh-oh."

Fowler nodded. "I heard the door behind me click shut."

Gasps went up, and somebody asked Fowler what he was wearing.

"Well, other than the anaconda," he replied with a smile, "just about nothing—a pair of torn Jockey shorts, soaking wet, because I'd been in the bathtub."

Fowler explained that he thought the elevator was his only chance—he could push the alarm button, or someone might come out who wouldn't panic and could get a bellhop. "I was on my way to the elevator, slumped as low to the floor as I could get and partially crouched next to the wall, when suddenly the elevator door opened. I heard this absolute barrage of giggles from the people in there, and out they came into the corridor—a girls' basketball team! It took a little time for it to sink in—that they were looking at a naked man dressed in a huge snake.

"I heard a couple of screams," Fowler said. "Then they were gone. Vanished. And they weren't the only ones. A couple of times, I got close to the elevator and didn't make it, because people would come out and scream and run. Finally, one of the hotel guys came up, and I was able to get back in my room."

Everyone leaned back. "Whew!" someone said.

Later, one of the guests said that he couldn't get Fowler's dilemma out of his mind. He kept thinking about the girls' basketball team. "What do you suppose those girls told their parents back in Fresno or Carson City or wherever?" he asked. "Do you think anyone believed them?"

"I doubt it" was the answer. "A naked man with a huge snake in the corridors of a luxury hotel in Burbank? I can just hear it: 'Now, dearie, eat your cereal. You just had a bad dream.' "

The New Yorker,
APRIL 22, 1996

Remembering Jackie

—

I suspect it's the last thing most people would think of, but I've always identified Jackie with pirates. When I first knew her, she seemed fixed on them. She once told me that as a child she had a pirate flag hanging on the wall of her room at Hammersmith Farm, in Newport. Her father looked like a pirate. She married a pirate, Ari Onassis.

But what comes to mind most vividly is a pirate party she gave at Hammersmith Farm one autumn afternoon in 1965 for her two children and their Newport friends—a collection of youthful Pells, Grosvenors, Drexels, Warrens, and Gardners, some young enough to be attending their first party. Jackie asked me to help organize it, though in fact she had already planned it very carefully in her own mind. The feature was a paper chase that would lead the children down sloping lawns to a treasure chest buried a few yards from the waters of Narragansett Bay. And her inspired notion was this: as soon as the children, having followed various clues, had reached the spot and begun digging for the chest, a boatload of adults dressed up as pirates would appear around the bend and come bustling ashore to reclaim their treasure. She had a list of pirates—six of us, as I recall, including Senator Claiborne Pell. There would be a fight, and the children would drive us back into the sea. "That's the scenario?" she said, phrasing her sentence in the form of a question, as she often did. She then said, "I have a longboat for you."

"A *longboat*?"

She laughed, and said that she'd called the Coast Guard station, and that they had agreed to lend her one for the occasion.

We went shopping together for the contents of the treasure chest. She nearly cleared out one gift shop we visited: strings of fake pearls; brass ashtrays; key chains. She got a treasure chest—a quite substantial one, with brass studs and a leather strap. I don't recall the exact circumstance of burying it, but I do remember that we put a rubber snake on top. She said, "As soon as the children see it, it will be time for you pirates to come around the rocks in your longboat. I'll signal you from shore."

Her enthusiasm, her childlike delight in all this, was irresistible. She wanted me to write a little story that she could read to the children the next day—a story of how the treasure came to be buried, and with hints of where the treasure might be found. Would I do this? Of course. I stayed up most of the night working on a kind of "diary" kept by one of the pirates.

On the day of the party, Jackie came with her paintbox and various items of clothing to sharpen us up as pirates. Once in the longboat, we stood on our oars as we waited for the signal from Jackie. I could see her, encircled by children, on the lawn up by the house. Then the children broke the cluster around her and, following the paper clues, eventually streamed toward the shoreline. At some point, shovels were produced. Soon enough the treasure chest was unearthed. Jackie waved us on.

The timing was perfect. I have often thought how terrifying the sight of us must have been to the children—we were waving our swords and shouting "Yo-ho-ho!" Some of the children turned and scampered off toward their mothers. Others sat and sobbed. Some were not so startled, though. I stepped off the bow of the longboat onto a shoreline boulder. There I was addressed by Caroline Kennedy, who was then about eight. "Well, I know who you are," she said, and stamped her foot.

The older children attacked us with shrill cries. We pirates succumbed gracefully and, I think, quite quickly. What sobbing there was subsided. But for Jackie the spirit of the afternoon was not quite done. She persuaded her Secret Service agent to walk the plank off Hammersmith Farm Dock. He went in with a tremendous splash.

At the end, close to sunset, I remember her in a circle of children. They asked her to read the diary to them again—as if to retain a bit more of that enchanted afternoon. The bell of her hair obscured her features as she bent over that absurd text. I could barely hear her voice as she whispered to them how something was going to come for them from the sea.

The New Yorker,
MAY 30, 1994

The Cellular Age

—

A man standing at the corner of Fifty-sixth and Lexington a few weeks ago waiting for the "Walk" sign to appear. Next to him was a woman who said very distinctly, "Margaret, I will have nothing to do with that man or his dog." Since only the two of them were waiting at the curb, he assumed that she was talking into a cellular phone. "How common it is these days," he said later, "to hear people chatting away in buses, or striding along the sidewalk talking quite loudly, apparently to themselves—behavior that, if it weren't for the little handheld sets, would be an easy ticket to the loony bin." He went on to say that he had looked over idly and was surprised to see that the woman was not holding a cellular phone but was, in fact, talking into a cupped hand held close to her ear, her little finger aloft in simulation of an antenna. 'That's right," he said. "She was carrying on an imaginary conversation into an imaginary phone."

That was not the end of it. When she caught him staring at her, she reached up with her free hand, folded the little finger—the "antenna"—down into her fist, and guided the whole into the pocket of her suit jacket. "What was surprising," the man said, "was that I had to hold back from apologizing for eavesdropping."

The New Yorker,
SEPTEMBER 16, 1996

In the Playpen of the Damned

—

The Las Vegas convention hall was packed with lines of men moving slowly toward the booths in which the porn stars were waiting: Tiffany Mynx, Kristi Myst, Misty Rain, Candy Apples, Sindee Coxx, Shyla Foxx, the Xs a salute to the X-rated industry in which they serve. The women were heavily made up with scarlet lips, mascaraed eyelashes, hair carefully coiffed and piled high, tight-fitting pants of black leather, some girls with tattoos (a butterfly, a black rose on a bare shoulder), and the shoes, of course, with the spike-like stiletto heels—hardly the girl-next-door look. Odd, because it seemed to perpetuate the concept that the porn star is only a notch or two up the social scale from the street prostitute. The stars came out of their booths and had pictures taken with their fans—the men's faces quite solemn, as if they were about to be handed a certificate for good citizenship. What they got was a poster. The girls rolled the posters into tight cylinders and then slid a rubber band up their length between thumb and forefinger—"like they're putting a condom on a guy," as someone in line pointed out.

I paid a visit to the booth of *AVN* (*Adult Video News*, the industry magazine that was sponsoring the 1997 porn-awards gala that would take place that evening), where I was introduced to a young woman who reviews porn movies for the publication (her nom de plume is Lily White). In addition, she has the gargantuan job of helping the staff select 300 nominees—from the staggering total of 7,200 porn films made over the year—for the silver statuettes that would be awarded later on. She was wearing a stud in her tongue and a ring in her nose. Sometimes, she said, she wears a silver spike through the septum of her nose. Her husband does her better—a big ring in the septum, a labret on either side of the lower lip, a ring in his right nipple, and the upper part of his body covered in tattoos. "In the supermarkets we kind of freak people out," she said.

"A certain amount of clashing when you kiss," I suggested.

"We feel quite uncomfortable without all that stuff on," she said. "It's like you lose your ballast."

We began talking about the night's awards ceremony. One hundred and one statuettes were to be given out. There were categories satisfying almost every imaginable delectation. She described the "Specialty" videos for those who like big-breasted women: *Big Boob Bikini Bash, The Duke of Knockers.* There was bondage, naturally: *The Punishment of Little Red Riding Hood.* Spanking: *Sweet Cheerleaders Spanked.* Bizarre Videos, which produced the spanking film, was also responsible for a nominee in what Lily referred to as the "Other Genre" category—*Waterworld: The Enema Movie*.

I remarked how numbing it must have been for her to plow through all this. Since the number of sexual positions and combinations is limited, wasn't pornography doomed to ultimate monotony? Lily agreed that the fast-forward button on the VCR is the essential piece of equipment in judging pornography . . . and that judicious use of it actually allowed her to get through one hundred or more films a day, since the sex acts themselves (often called "commercials") were invariably filmed at close range and unremittingly, as if the cameraman had set his camera onto a small tripod at the foot of the bed and gone off to have himself a beer. Fast-forward time.

"The formula is two minutes between commercials," Lily was saying.

I mentioned that I'd learned of a nice sixteenth-century word for "commercial": a "flourish."

"A what?"

"A 'flourish,' as in, 'Let's have a flourish on the tilting green.' "

Lily laughed and said that whether it was a "commercial" or a "flourish," it was still fast-forward time.

I was surprised to learn later that an *AVN* compatriot of hers named Jim Holliday (who's famous around the magazine's offices for outfitting himself entirely in white, including his moccasins, and who bears the title "senior historian") would have been horrified at Lily's use of the fast-forward button. A porn-film anthologist as well as a director, he writes in an introduction to his *Adult Video Almanac and Trivia Treasury* that he never fast-forwarded once during his viewing of almost two thousand films while researching material for his book. He claims that "[a]ll sex scenes are not the same, and fast-forwarding can cause you to miss a milestone of erotica found in an otherwise dreadful film. I will put up with the dreary agony just to find those gems."

When I met Holliday, he mentioned a number of times that he had the mind-set of an Ohio farm boy, which was his upbringing: "Quite normal," he said. His insistence was that the intent of pornography, whether written or pictorial, was to arouse sexual feelings—not to entertain. He makes up for a lack of plot by populating his films with large numbers of stars—ergo, more couplings. He specializes in eighteen-to-thirty-girl epics with such titles as *Sorority Sex Kittens* and *Car Wash Angels.* He makes a lot of what he calls "double-vocational-adjective" movies—as in *Cheerleader Nurses, Sorority Nurses,* etc. The success of these has led predictably to "return" films . . . *The Return of the Cheerleader Nurses.* He mentioned a possible ne plus ultra in this field: *The Return of the Black Anal Sorority Cheerleader Nurses.* His *Car Wash Angels* would be in contention that night.

He took me over to another booth and presented me to a slight, middle-aged man, Alex de Renzy, considered one of the titan filmmakers of the porn industry. I knew something about him. In 1969 he had gone to Denmark with a two-man crew and filmed Copenhagen's sex fair, where there was considerable flaunting in public of what hadn't been seen anywhere before. De Renzy spent eight days making a documentary about the Danish porn industry, which eventually showed in mainstream movie theaters in the United States. We had met before. In fact, jokingly, I had asked him at the time if he could slip me into one of his films, an interesting participatory exercise. He seemed so agreeable that I stammered about and told him that if he happened to be filming in Egypt, I'd be glad to oblige.

"Do you remember that?" I asked. "I specified it had to be Egypt."

"I never understood that."

"I don't either," I said.

Shouts rose from down the aisle; porn stars were tossing condom packages to the men waiting in line. I wandered over to look at some of the booths featuring bondage and S&M devices—leather whips, paddles, ankle restraints, studded halters, love cuffs, stiletto-heeled boots that looked more like weapons than footwear, women's edible undies (retail price: $1.75), biker caps, bitch-goddess bras, chokers, leashes, harnesses. The most alarming device was on display in the Paradise Electro Stimulations booth—the Auto Erotic Chair, a grim, skeletal black-leather structure that at first glance suggested an offshoot of an electric chair. A flier I was handed announced that it was "a new apex in bondage gear . . . four top-quality leather restraints, which with the fully adjustable arm and leg horns will get you or your other 'spread eagle' in no time." Two "electro stimulative devices" come with the chair—the Vaginal Plug (which can be "aimed for a perfect fit") and the Micro Acrylic Anal Plug (no mention of whether this could be "aimed" or not).

As I was walking away, a gentleman leaned out of a booth and called out my name. He introduced himself as Bill Margold and quickly announced himself as a Detroit Lions fan. His calling card, which he pressed on me, was trimmed in blue and silver, the Lions' colors. It read "WILLIAM MARGOLD CREATED HIMSELF." We talked about the Lions. He's worried about their defense. We could have been chatting in the Silverdome in Pontiac. Margold is such a fan that he has incorporated mention of the Detroit Lions into most of the three hundred porn films he told me he has made to date. "Is there anything better than sex?" a girl asks him as the two lie exhausted on a bed in one of his early films. "Yes," he replies. "Watching the Detroit Lions play." In one film, Margold used the stage name Lem Lary, derived from Lem Barney and Yale Lary, two of Detroit's stars in the sixties and seventies. "Do the Lions know this?" I asked, wondering how William Ford, the team's owner, a mild-mannered family man, would take to this symbiotic relationship.

"Oh, yes," Margold said. "I get fine seats for the games. Hey, you know what?"

"What?"

"You're responsible for my getting into the porn industry."

I looked at him, dumbfounded.

"That's right. You were my inspiration." He went on to say that in 1968 he had reviewed my book *Paper Lion* for the *Santa Monica Evening Outlook.* He looked at me and laughed. He said, "I knew *you* weren't going to get into the business." (I was tempted to interrupt and tell him about Alex de Renzy and Egypt but refrained.) "So I said to myself, *Why not try it?* If I failed, it would be a comic tragedy and I'd have a great story. If I succeeded . . . if I could pull off the three Gs . . ."

"The three Gs?"

"Get up, get in, get off . . . and do this on cue. I succeeded. My first film was *The Goddaughter.* Others followed. *Weekend Fantasy. Lust Inferno.* I went into the playpen of the damned. That's right. Once you do this, you're damned forever. But I didn't want to get out. I knew I could become the leading authority. I didn't come into it for the sexual activity. That's mechanical. I came into it for the glory."

I was to learn that Margold is not only committed but also a substantial figure in the porn industry—known as Papa Bear for his efforts to help his "kids" work out their personal problems, especially concerns of self-esteem. His apartment in West Hollywood is overrun with stuffed teddy bears sent to him in gratitude. He has been in all aspects of the industry. As an agent, he discovered one of the most famous of porn stars: Seka. "I told her, 'I'm starting you off as hamburger. You'll end up filet mignon.' " He is fond of aphorisms. His most famous is probably "No one ever died of an overdose of pornography."

—

That evening, the ballroom of the Riviera Hotel filled with people. The men in the orchestra onstage wore dinner jackets. The master of ceremonies was Bobby Slayton, a stand-up comedian, who after each joke would turn to the orchestra and motion to the drummer for a rim shot—ker-*boom.* Slayton shared the stage with a number of "cohostesses," including a tall, graceful porn star in a white sheath dress named Nici Sterling, who is from England, where the pornography industry is a shadowy presence—no adult stores; clerks in dingy Soho alleys keep unmarked videos under the counter. She warmed up the crowd by remarking that there was more to the English than a stiff upper lip. Slayton later countered this with the comment "Englishwomen don't come; they arrive." Ker-*boom.*

The awards procedure involved as many as seven porn stars, almost always women, walking out in single file from the wings to a microphone at center stage. Each in turn would read out a nominee's name from a list. After the envelope was opened, the seven girls would lean toward the mike and attempt to call out the winner in unison—very rarely successfully. It was not easy for them to sing out as one, "And the winner is . . . *Buttslammer 2!*"

Unlike at the Oscars, no film clips of the award winners were shown on a giant screen—predictable enough, I suppose, since no matter how jaundiced, or how supportive of the X-rated industry, it is hard to imagine that the audience members viewing, say, the

Best Spanking scene would not have erupted into a bedlam of hooting and catcalling.

The award, held high in triumph by the winners, was a "Winged Victory" statuette of a woman holding aloft a wreath—a trophy that could just as well have been bestowed upon the champions of the local girls' softball league. The female winners, perched on their stiletto heels, moved for the podium in staccato strides. Once there, they found that they had very little to say . . . a "gosh," often followed by a fit of giggling. Out front we were spared what Oscar audiences are forced to suffer—the list of people "I would like to thank," on and on. It occurred to me that because of the vast number of films in which each winner had performed over the course of a year, much less the number of lovers, it was hopeless to sort out a few names for special mention.

A male star named T. T. Boy received an award for his performance in a video called *Shock*. Often called simply "the Boy," he is a legend in the business, not only for being able to maintain an erection indefinitely (which in the industry is known as "sustaining wood") but also for producing an ejaculation (referred to as a "money shot," a "cum shot," a "money pop," etc.) on cue—and, amazingly, for being able to do a number of them in succession. In *Sorority Sex Kittens*, he produced five money pops in one scene. T. T. Boy does not look at all glamorous—he's a small, tough-guy, assistant-mobster type; sometimes he chews gum during his lovemaking scenes. He pounds his partners. From the podium he said he hadn't seen *Shock* (he plays a gargoyle) but heard it was interesting. Once memorably described as "nothing more than a life-support system for his penis," he got the kind of admiring, solid applause reserved for a large artillery piece going by in a parade.

My friend Holliday didn't think much of T. T. Boy's gargoyle footage. "I'm a Midwestern farm boy from Ohio," he told me again. "Gargoyles? They're to jump down and slit someone's throat, not make love. Gargoyles belong in horror films."

"What about T. T. Boy himself?"

"One of a kind. In the whole business there are only about sixteen or twenty men who can perform—the paladins of Charlemagne!" he said grandly.

The big winner of the night was a cute young star named Missy, sometimes referred to as the Shirley Temple of the industry. She won both the Best New Starlet and the Female Performer of the Year awards—a "historic event," as it was reported later in *AVN*. Missy, who seemed to me more a healthy-cheerleader type than a Shirley Temple, thanked her husband, Mickey, for his support during her "sexual adventure." I wondered if Mickey didn't deserve an award for Most Open-minded. At our table we worked it out that, in the forty films she had made in her first year in the business (given that she had performed in, say, four commercials, or flourishes, in each), Missy had been unfaithful to Mickey 160 times. Someone at the table pointed out that Mickey was a porn star himself. Out came a pad and pencil. If Mickey had made as many films as his wife, averaging two partners per, the total number of acts of infidelity would amount to 240, a figure surely of *Guinness Book of World Records* proportions.

Missy stayed onstage and was joined by all the evening's winners and performers. A comedian arrived and, quite off-key, sang, "Thank heaven for grown-up girls." This was followed by the porn stars' doing a lively macarena (announced as a "cockeranal"), in which the hand movements included a move from the crotch to the mouth. The dancing became disorganized, a lot of kissing and mock lovemaking. Many of the principals were not wearing anything under their dresses. Then everybody clustered together and, arranging themselves like a family portrait, sang, "We're a lovely horny porno family." The lights went up and it was over.

I left for the Hotel Rio, where I was told there was going to be a cyber-orgy. I had no idea what that was, but I went anyway. The party was held in a duplex suite on the twentieth floor. The place was crowded with men. I didn't see any women. But they were expected. From the second floor of the suite, I could look down over a balcony at the crowd milling below. Not far away was Paul Thomas, the porn star and director, sitting alone. One of Charlemagne's paladins!

It was my chance. I thought I'd ask him why the female stars invariably wear high-heeled shoes during the flourishes in X-rated movies. In the early days of pornographic films, the men often wore calf-length black stockings and the women wore high-heeled shoes, as if both partners felt they had to maintain at least some shred of dignity. But in present-day films, only the high heels remain; the stilettos, pitch-black, wave above the male performer's back like a set of antennae. The insistence on heels leads to rather improbable scenes—the female star tottering on spike heels as she heads for a liaison in a forest glade, or a poolside cabana, or a barn, or a garage (a favorite venue) to perform with a guy against the flank of a motorcycle. The shoes never come off.

I went over and introduced myself. We sat and chatted. He told me something about himself. A graduate of the University of Wisconsin, he had gone to New York seeking a career in acting. Blessed with movie-star good looks, he had appeared onstage in both *Hair* and *Jesus Christ Superstar.* He said he had been attracted to the porn world because he liked the exhibitionist factor. He liked being watched.

"So I got a chance to be in the Mitchell Brothers' X-rated *Autobiography of a Flea.* I didn't know what I was doing. I was a drugged-out hippie. I wanted to show my penis to everybody, and it was a perfect opportunity. I was a swinger. My generation had a much larger range of sexual experience—swapping partners, tripping on acid, watching your girlfriend with a bunch of people in the balcony, and partying all night in Polk Street in San Francisco and everybody having sex . . . that was what was going on."

I said I didn't remember that part about the guys up in the balcony. . . .

"Oh, yes."

He got up and looked down at the crowd, and then turned back and shrugged.

"No sign of the cyber-orgy?"

"Nope."

He sat down and continued. "I'm telling you that in all likelihood I might have made it in the mainstream as an actor or a director. But doing X-rated films will ruin your chances in the mainstream. You'll never enter big-time corporate America. You'll probably never run for president."

Playpen of the damned, I thought. I asked if he was recognized on the street.

"Every day. I like it."

Thomas made hundreds of films. Now he works as a director for Vivid Video, which since 1987 has had a subsidiary contract with Playboy Enterprises. He is able to make $150,000-budget X-rated films because of the edited versions—removal of any sight of male genitalia or penetration—which appear on pay-cable networks and on hotel-bedroom TV screens.

Thomas is one of the few people who still shoots on film rather than with video. "I tell a story," he explained. "I try to involve the audience in the characters of the story so that when it comes time for them to have sex, it means a bit more to the audience. They have some emotion invested in what's going on. I'm also wary of porn conventions," he said. "Big hair, big breasts. We don't have a makeup person on the set. We hire girls with natural breasts."

"What's your take on having girls wear high-heeled shoes in bed?"

To my surprise, he liked the convention.

"They extend the leg," he said simply.

"I talked to a guy, a porn star named Nick East, who said he got gouged."

"His problem."

We gazed on the men milling about below, many of them facing the door through which the stars were expected to appear.

I stirred and said, "Paul, did you know that back in the sixteenth century having sex was sometimes called having a flourish?"

"Is that right?" he replied. "A flourish."

"It turns up in the diaries of the time. 'We had a flourish on the settee.' "

"I like it. I'm going to use it."

Think of that, I said to myself. . . . I had made two contributions to the porn industry—Bill Margold and now "flourish."

It was getting late. It didn't look as though the cyber-orgy was going to take place, certainly not in our suite, or even that any of the porn stars would show up for a drink.

I thanked Thomas for taking time to chat with me. Out in the hotel corridor I spotted T. T. Boy walking by, moving swiftly, a small entourage crowding around him . . . like a prizefighter on the way to the ring. On his way to the cyber-orgy? I didn't hasten after him.

In my hotel room, the TV set was on. I could watch an adult film for $9.95. It would have been appropriate enough, I suppose. But I didn't. The next day I heard that a girl at the party had performed with a beer bottle and danced naked on a table. At the time I was sound asleep.

Men's Journal,
NOVEMBER 1998

It's a Bird! It's a Plane! It's a Whiskey Submarine!

—

The young woman taking me around Washington, D.C., on my book tour this fall was the one who mentioned the submarine. She was telling me that the Russian navy had offered to sell one to Tom Clancy, the bestselling author of *The Hunt for Red October*, a thriller about a Russian commander who defects with his submarine to the West. "Come on, now," I said. "A submarine?" She was insistent. "They wanted him to pay for it. He's sold so many books he can pay for *anything*."

It was her impression that Clancy wanted to keep the submarine moored to a dock just off his waterfront property on Chesapeake Bay. He could fix it up, and maybe put a Ping-Pong table in for the kids. Wonderful playground for a rainy day! Apparently, though, his wife hadn't approved.

I had a quick mental image of Mrs. Clancy, undoubtedly a sensible woman whose idea of landscaping was more traditional—gladiolas, a clipped hedge, and perhaps a tastefully constructed birdbath—and who would stamp her foot at the thought of a submarine moored at the bottom of the garden.

"The Clancys have a shooting range in the cellar," my guide was saying.

"Hmm." My mental image of Mrs. Clancy changed somewhat. How could she condone all that shooting going on in the basement and still object to a submarine moored at dockside?

The other bestselling author I know who has an interest in owning a submarine is Kurt Vonnegut, who is my next-door neighbor in Sagaponack, Long Island. Early in the summer mornings we often meet on the short walk to the little Sagaponack general store to pick up the morning paper. On the way, we chat like housewives about domestic problems. One day he told me that mourning doves were up on his roof, cocking their heads and looking at him in his bath through the bathroom-ceiling skylight. He had designed the skylight himself and sometimes, under the piercing scrutiny of the birds, cooing and shifting about with their claws scratching on the glass to get a better view, he wishes he hadn't. He said to me one morning, "I have a toad," and I knew he was not talking about a toad in his swimming pool, or in the garden, or anything, but that he had one splay-footed on the skylight glass, looking in along with the mourning doves.

Another domestic problem we discuss is the plague of radio-controlled model airplanes overhead on weekends. A model-airplane club has the use of a small grass strip on Foster's farm just down the road. Sometimes three or four of them are in the air at the same time—the whine of their tiny engines incessant and infuriating. Some of the models are very fancy—biplanes, imitation Fokkers—and they do clever maneuvers: loops, stalls, Immelmanns. Sometimes one will do lazy, everlasting circles as if the owner, sitting on the grass down the road with the control box in his lap, is so entranced by the thought of the artificial extension of his own being in the sky that he doesn't do anything too risky for fear of tumbling his plane into the potato fields.

So Kurt and I, on our stroll to the general store, discuss what we can do about this. Vonnegut's fanciful solution is to have a submarine rise from the bottom of his swimming pool to fire off a salvo of heat-seeking surface-to-air missiles. Above, a perky model plane, its wings glistening in the sunlight, would suddenly disintegrate in a puff of fine powder like a shattered clay pigeon. At this point the submarine would blow its tanks to submerge and sink silently down to rest next to the drainpipe.

My own solution is far less fanciful. It involves falcons. I would let one loose to rise out of the honeysuckle hedgerows and beat up to a point in the sky, just barely visible, and then dive on a plane as it poised at the top of a loop-the-loop to spin it out of the air, fluttering it down to the potato fields, its engine mute.

Actually, the use of falcons was suggested to me by a friend who came to stay for the weekend in Sagaponack. He's a falconer himself. He once trained a great horned owl. He was sitting by the pool, squinting at the planes circling over Foster's farm.

"I'd like to fly Jessie Anne out of the hood to drop one of those," he said.

"What's that mean?" I asked.

"That means to slip a bird when the quarry's in sight," he said. That day by the pool, he told me a story—a few weeks before, when he was just about to board a flight from Abidjan to Frankfurt, he had been bounced from first class to coach. An elegant type, he had complained and made quite a nuisance of himself. Sulking in his coach seat, he couldn't resist finding out who had replaced him. He walked up the aisle and peeked through the curtains that separated first class from coach.

"No one was sitting there," he said. "But on top of each headrest was perched a hooded falcon—sixteen of them."

He went on to say that when the plane banked steeply to land, the curtains swayed open and he could see the double lines of falcons each adjusting to the slant. By this time he had discovered that a Saudi prince on his way to hunt in the Black Forest had traveled in his own private jet and had sent his falcons by way of public transportation.

"Perfectly natural," my friend said. "I apologized to everyone I could for making such a fuss. If I'd only known," he said.

Vonnegut and I are not the only Sagaponack residents concerned about the airplanes. Bob Dash, the well-known artist, lives just in back of the Vonneguts and across a lane from us. His extensive gardens are one of the showplaces of the area. He takes garden clubs on tours on the weekends, speaking loudly above the whine of the planes overhead. I asked him if a plane had ever crashed there. "Venomous things!" he exclaimed. "A wing came off one of them and almost killed my accountant."

"What did you do with it?"

"The wing? Well, I picked it up and walked over to Foster's farm. There, just across the fence, was my mechanic. That's the *trouble,*" he went on. "The people who fly those planes are your electricians, your mechanics, your plumbers. If you complain, you're suddenly without water, without lights, you can't start your car. . . ."

I told Dash about my scheme with falcons. He suggested I get much larger birds—emus, ostriches—big birds that would stride out and storm on the control boxes. He thought the Vonnegut submarine was a splendid idea. "Comes up, shoots them out of the sky, and then disappears. Who would guess?"

So last week I called Tom Clancy, not only to satisfy my curiosity about his own submarine but to ask him—as an expert—what he might suggest for Kurt Vonnegut's swimming pool. I introduced myself and said I'd heard that the Russians had offered to sell him a submarine.

"Close," he said. He went on to explain that a friend of his, until recently a naval attaché in Moscow, had heard that the Russians were selling off their Whiskey-class subs, thirty years old and obsolete.

"How much for one sub?" I asked.

"About one hundred thousand dollars."

I whistled, and said that didn't seem very much. "What do you get for that?"

"A thirty-year-old obsolete submarine."

"I mean, do they throw in a torpedo or two, the ship's clock, and everything?"

"You get about a thousand tons of steel. Melt that down and you get an awful lot of razor blades. My friend had an idea to use these subs as theme-park restaurants, sort of like the railroad diners. He wanted me to go in as a partner. Borscht on the menu.

"Actually, it's not such a new idea," Clancy went on. "Some years ago a Whiskey-class sub ran onto the rocks off Sweden and got stuck . . . remember that? Big international incident. Whiskey on the rocks. Afterward, a Swedish entrepreneur got hold of one and used it as a centerpiece for a shopping mall."

I was disappointed that he hadn't wanted a submarine for himself—my Washington guide apparently had it wrong.

"But they were willing to sell you one?"

"Oh, yes," Clancy said. "They need the money. Besides, the Russian military people like me. I treat them realistically."

"How large is one of these subs?"

He looked it up for me. Perhaps not surprisingly, he has reference books of that kind close at hand. "Two hundred and forty-seven feet, six inches long."

"Much longer than a swimming pool."

"Considerably."

"What about midget submarines?"

Clancy said he didn't know much about them. He'd seen interesting early models in England designed for coastal defense. "Turn-of-the-century jobs."

"One last question," I said. I could feel Clancy getting on edge at the other end. He kept telling me he was trying to get his family ready for a trip to Disneyland.

"What about a sub's surface-to-air capacity? Just idle curiosity," I added.

Clancy said: "The Russians are working on an SAM rigged next to the periscope. It's really to scare someone up there in a plane—make them keep their distance. After all, the number-one consideration for a submarine is not to be discovered."

"Exactly," I said.

Not long after, I ran into Vonnegut at a party. I edged him into a corner. "I've been conferring with Clancy," I whispered.

"Who?"

"Tom Clancy. And Bob Dash."

"Oh, yes," Kurt said. He looked puzzled. He reached for a cigarette.

"The airplane business," I whispered.

"Oh, yes." Kurt said he'd seen one recently through his bathroom skylight.

"I've been working on the submarine project," I went on. "We may have to resort to midgets!" I shouted at him over the growing uproar of the party.

"Midgets?"

"Midget submarines." I told him we'd probably have to enlarge the pool. Bob Dash could supply the shovels.

Vonnegut looked preoccupied. "Hey," he said. "I've been down to Foster's farm, checking it out. Their girls sit inside the cars and gossip . . . like the wives of jazz musicians . . . couldn't care less. Maybe they know the radio frequencies these guys use. Get this out of them and maybe we can lock into their controls."

"Fly 'em into each other!" I shouted.

" . . . Throw the kill switch."

"You'll have to infiltrate," I said. "Become a mole. It's spy stuff. I should be talking to John le Carré, not Clancy."

Vonnegut leaned forward and whispered in my ear. "Let me know what he says."

Esquire,
FEBRUARY 1991

My Olympic Trials

—

Everyone must wonder wistfully if there isn't something other than what they actually practice in their lives (playing in a yacht-club tennis tournament) at which they would be incredibly adept if they could only find out what it was—that a paintbrush worked across a canvas for the first time would indicate an amazing talent. Or that one would rise from a minor position at the executive board meeting table and address the CEOs with a proposal so illuminating that around the rim of the mahogany table the officers of the company would rise and applaud. If an idiot savant could sit down at a piano and suddenly bat out a Chopin étude, wasn't the same sort of potential locked up somewhere in all of us?

I have always wondered (less so, I must admit, as the years have gone by) if there wasn't some extraordinary athletic skill lurking within my body of which I was not aware—as if by chance on some athletic field I had picked up a javelin and thrown it, just to try, and through some perfect and startling alchemic convulsion of muscles the thing had sailed an eighth of a mile and stuck quivering in the earth. Astonished observers would ask to see it done again. Why not? After a few more titanic tosses, just to show that a fluke was not involved and of course surprising myself in the process, I would be urged to call the U.S. Olympic Committee. "Ahem," I planned to say when I got an authority on the line, "I've just discovered the most extraordinary thing about myself. I am a javelin thrower."

Unlike others who share such absurd Walter Mitty daydreams, I had actually done something about it. A month before the Olympic Games in 1984, I had gone to the Olympic Training Center under the shadow of Pikes Peak in Colorado Springs to be tested in the sports physiology laboratories to see if by chance there was a particular Olympic event (after all, there are over two hundred of them) for which I was perfectly adapted. I planned to write a piece about their findings.

A number of teams were in training at the Center when I arrived. I looked at them speculatively—judo (no chance there—too specialized), boxing (no, wrong-shaped nose), race-walkers (not dignified enough on the move), water-polo players, their nose clips dangling from their necks (a possibility?), and then out above the training fields I spotted the occasional arc of a javelin on the wing.

My testers were Dr. Jackie Puhl, a young vibrant woman with a Ph.D. in exercise physiology from Kent State, who rides a bicycle ten miles a day to her job at the Center, and Bob Hintermeister, a lean sprinter type who earned his degree in physical education at the University of Massachusetts. Dr. Puhl said: "A lot of what we can offer from here is a kind of support system for your coach so he can get a theoretical optimization of your athletic abilities."

"I don't have a coach," I said.

"Oh."

After a pause, I said, "Maybe I can get a coach after you tell me what I can do best."

I spent the day moving from one instrument to the next. I sat down and pulled at the sawed-off oars of a Concept II rowing ergometer. I submitted myself to a Biokinetic Pacer bench unit. I performed on a Quinton 18-72 treadmill, breathing hard into a hoselike attachment called a Gould programmable electric ergometer. At each station, computer screens glowed with figures, and printouts emerged, many with finely etched graphs. I was strapped into the Cybex II isokinetic dynamometer to measure the strength of my arms and legs. The Cybex (I was told) can show if an athlete has a muscle imbalance—whether the right leg is stronger than the left, in which case the balance can be redressed with the proper exercise. "This will tell if I tilt when I walk," I said. "Possibly," Mr. Hintermeister said.

The first indication of excitement on the part of my testers came with an exercise called the fev 1.0, which measures how much air can be forcefully blown out in one second. "Fev 1.0" stands for "Forced Expiratory Volume" at one second.

"It is really a very sharp curve," Hintermeister said, looking at the graph. "It's almost as if . . . you blew up balloons for a living." He looked at me questioningly.

"Well, I blow up the usual four or five a year," I told him. "Birthday parties. I can tell you that the cheaper the balloon the more difficult it is to inflate. The really cheap ones tend to escape the lips and flail around the room. Right?"

One test I skipped—which was to have some muscle removed to tell whether I was a slow or fast twitcher. I didn't like the looks of the instrument that does this—a cylinder about the size of a large fountain pen. It contains a guillotine-like contraption that snips off a piece of muscle so its fibers can be inspected through a microscope. The procedure leaves a small scar, perhaps a centimeter in length. What is learned by going through this is whether one has a high percentage of fast-twitch muscle fibers, which means one's muscular makeup is suitable for anaerobic activities such as weight lifting or the one-hundred-yard dash, where gulps of oxygen are not at a premium, or slow-twitch, which indicates aerobic activities in which lungs full of oxygen are required, such as kayaking or running a marathon.

I have since regretted not having this done—if only for the scar. A scar, even a small one that must be searched for, is worth having for conversational gambits. "See this here. Got it trying out for the Olympics. Showed I was a fast [or slow] twitcher."

At the end of my session Jackie Puhl collected the printouts and the data sheets and we gathered around a conference table. "Have any patterns emerged?" I asked. "There are," Dr. Puhl replied, "two interesting oddities about your charts." My heart jumped.

"First of all, which is very unusual, your hamstrings—that is to say the muscles in the back of your thighs—are far more powerful than the quadricep muscles in the front, those four muscular bands we call quads. Very unusual."

"What does it mean?"

"It means that you can kick backward more powerfully than you can kick forward."

"Oh."

"Then your fev 1.0 test," Dr. Puhl went on, "shows that you're very adept at expelling air swiftly. Snorting."

"What is this good for? Does an Olympic event come to mind?"

"This backward kicking motion might come in handy riding a horse," Dr. Puhl said. "Spurring him on."

Hintermeister came up with a comment. "It's too bad football isn't on the Olympic agenda," he said. "You could kick field goals backward."

Dr. Puhl shuffled her papers and continued. "As for being able to blow out sharply, I just don't know. With swimmers, of course, it's helpful to be able to exhale abruptly, but the rest of your tests don't suggest the water's your medium. I'm quite at a loss, frankly."

Some months later a somewhat caustic friend of mine—to whom I had described the Colorado Springs findings—was ingenious enough to offer an activity that smartly combined both skills.

"That combination of kicking backward, pawing at the ground," he said, "and snorting sharply, brings only one thing to mind. And that's the bullfight." He paused. "That's where you belong, the bullring, and it's not the matador I have in mind!"

from *The X Factor*,
1990

Wish List

I'd like to be able to do tricks with a golf ball—to flip the ball off the green with my putter and catch it. I've seen a number of professional golfers do this in match play; the nonchalance with which they do it is truly enviable. I'd also like to be able to pop a ball up and down off a pitching wedge, over and over—not necessarily to fungo it into the distance like Tiger Woods, but just to have this insouciant skill of hand. I'd like to have Britney Spears stop mid-gyration on the stage, notice me in the front row, and cry out, "It's you!" On the gym floor, just goofing around, I'd like to throw the ball over my shoulder into the basket and hear someone say, "Wow, he has a real sense of where the basket is." I'd like to crouch in the curve of a great tsunami and run my hand through the sea wall off my shoulder. I'd like to have a snappy moniker: Wolf, or Moose, or something as memorable as Joltin' Joe, or the Splinter . . . or the Elephant, as in "Hey! Hey! It's the Elephant!" I'd like to throw a perfect spiral, just once, so the front of the ball is a dot, the leather revolving around it. I'd like to bowl a perfect game. I'd like to arch into the water without making a splash, the wake of my passage down the lane as I do the butterfly washing over the lip of the pool. "Is that Mark Spitz?" I'd like to slide the tips of my skis over the sill of a precipice, look down at the village far below, and, just before pushing off, hear a woman in form-fitting ski clothes cry out, "Don't go! It's too steep!" Nothing wrong with crossing the blue line, the puck nicely on the stick, with only the goalie to beat. And I wish I could throw a knuckleball. I'd like to have it come to me one afternoon, perhaps while I'm throwing the ball to my son, a ball without motion so that it ducks and dances . . . and take that thing to spring training. "Ahem. I have something I think you might like to take a look at."

There are many more, and the splendid thing is that they are all available—as soon as the hour is late and the fire has gone down and it is time to drift off into sleep. It's only a matter of picking one before the sweet darkness arrives.

Men's Journal,
NOVEMBER 2002

Arcadia

—

An island. Something along the lines of the Seychelles—with a coastline of granite rocks, like Henry Moore sculptures rising out of a warm tropical sea.

A few incidentals: a large and perfectly balanced boomerang, some bright-colored bathtub toys with small propellers and keys to wind them up, the ingredients and tools for making and setting off large aerial fireworks (along with an instruction booklet), athletic equipment, and a substantial amount of fishing gear, including a number of small red and white bobs.

The island compound would feature a dining pavilion among the palm trees, or a hall, rather, a somewhat baronial edifice with excellent acoustics, so that conversations, even very whispery ones, would not drift up into the rafters and get lost among the ceremonial flags. On hand would be an excellent butler, quite deaf, but faithful, and willing to help with the fireworks.

The compound would contain a number of guesthouses. These small mushroomlike structures, set apart from each other, would all have views of the sea. They would be well appointed inside, each one having a white fan turning slowly on the ceiling and a large porcelain washbasin with a neatly folded, fluffed-up towel alongside. Every afternoon I would know my guests were being installed into these accommodations by the sounds of the houseboys chattering excitedly among themselves as they carried the baggage from the quay.

I would not see my guests before dinner, my own day being quite somnolent. Oh, a little boomerang tossing, perhaps, the construction of an aerial bomb or two, some bait-casting in the mangrove swamps, and surely a bit of a tub before dinner. (It's not that I would feel unfriendly toward my guests, simply that my personal pursuits, especially sitting in a tub winding up a small blue tugboat, would not be especially conducive to their companionship.)

The guest list would be composed of people I have never met. Not only that, they would be dead. Ludwig II, the mad king of Bavaria, dined alone with busts of various dignitaries—Louis XIV and Marie Antoinette among them—set on chairs down the length of the banquet hall at Linderhof, and carried on an animated if slightly one-sided conversation with them. My guests would be the real shades.

Many of them would be seagoing people—the captain of the deserted brigantine *Mary Celeste;* Joshua Slocum, who also disappeared at sea; Richard Haliburton, who may have fallen off the stern of a Chinese junk; and Captain Kidd, to discuss the whereabouts of his vanished treasure. Schubert, to inquire about the "Lost Symphony," and perhaps to persuade him to play a bit on the stand-up Yamaha in the corner.

Some of my dinner partner choices would be more quixotic. I've always wanted to know why Thomas Cromwell, Oliver's great-uncle, was so anxious to get Henry VIII to marry Anne, the daughter of the duke of Cleves. (The king took one look and hated her. The marriage took place but was never consummated, and Cromwell lost his head. Frightful error of judgment.) So, he could have a brandy or two at dinner and perhaps give an odd little talk on matchmaking. And General James Longstreet. Why, I would ask, did he not roll up Cemetery Ridge when he had the chance?

I don't know how much of this it would be possible to take. So my Arcadia would also have a swift means of escape—preferably a drug-runner's cigarette boat with a deep rumble of a motor in it, which, after a time, would tie up at a New York pier where, waiting in a fine mist, there would be a yellow cab.

Harper's Magazine,
NOVEMBER 2003

About the Author

George Plimpton was the originator of "participatory journalism" and was the editor of *The Paris Review*. His books include *Paper Lion, Out of My League, The Bogey Man, Open Net, The Curious Case of Sidd Finch,* and oral biographies of Edie Sedgwick and Truman Capote.

About the Type

This book was set in Electra, a typeface designed for Linotype by W. A. Dwiggins, the renowned type designer (1880–1956). Electra is a fluid typeface, avoiding the contrasts of thick and thin strokes that are prevalent in most modern typefaces.